Sasanian Coins and History

The Civic Numismatic Collection of Milan

Sasanika Series, No. 3

The purpose of this series is to publish scholarly works related to Sasanian civilization in the fields of history, philology, literature, art and archaeology.

No. 1
Touraj Daryaee
Sasanian Iran (224-651 CE): Portrait of a Late Antique Empire
(2008)

No. 2
Evangelos Venetis, Touraj Daryaee,
and Massoumeh Alinia
Bibliographica Sasanika: A Bibliographical Guide to Sasanian Iran
Volume I: Years 1990-99
(2009)

Published under the auspices of
Dr. Samuel M. Jordan Center for Persian Studies and Culture
University of California, Irvine

Sasanian Coins and History

The Civic Numismatic Collection of Milan

Andrea Gariboldi

MAZDA PUBLISHERS   Costa Mesa   California
2010

Mazda Publishers, Inc.
Academic publishers since 1980
P.O. Box 2603, Costa Mesa, California 92628 U.S.A.
www.mazdapub.com
A. K. Jabbari, Publisher

Library of Congress Cataloging-in-Publication Data

Gariboldi, Andrea.
[Monetazione sasanide nelle Civiche raccolte numismatiche
di Milano. English]
Sasanian Coinage and History : The Civic Numismatic Collection of Milan /
by Andrea Gariboldi.
p. cm. — (Sasanika series ; no. 3)
Translation of La monetazione sasanide nelle Civiche raccolte numismatiche di
Milano.
Includes bibliographical references and index.

ISBN 13: 978-1-56859-252-7 (alk. paper)
ISBN 10: 1-56859-252-3

1. Coins, Sassanid—Italy—Milan—Catalogs. 2. Money—Iran—History—To
1500. 3. Civiche raccolte numismatiche di Milano—Catalogs. I. Title.
CJ1363.G3713 2010
737.4945'211—dc22
2010031564

انتشارات مزدا

Acknowledgement

The board of editors of Sasanika Series would like to thank the Adel Aali Foundation for its support.

CONTENTS

Preface

Dr. Andrea Gariboldi's book is not only a study of the sixty nine Sasanian coins at the Milan Museum but also a good introductory handbook to the study of Sasanian numismatics and history. The publication of the series on ancient Iran is due to the support of Dr. Samuel M. Jordan Center for Persian Studies and Culture at the University of California, Irvine in association with *Sasanika: Late Antique Near East Project*, *Adel Aali Foundation*, and the *Iranica Institute*. I wish to thank Dr. Nasrin Rahimieh, Director of the Center for Persian Studies, and Dr. A. Kamron Jabbari, President of Mazda Publishers for making the publication of this series possible.

Touraj Daryaee
Howard C. Baskerville Professor in the History of Iran and the Persianate World

Sasanian Coins in
the Civic Numismatic Collection of Milan

1.1 The History of the Collection and Criteria of the Catalogue.

The collection of the Sasanian coins in the *Civico Gabinetto Numismatico* in Milan is composed of sixty-nine coins made of silver.[1] Even if this collection could not be considered a great one, due to the exiguous number of the coins, it should be taken into consideration because it includes coins which refer almost to the entire Sasanian period, from the coming to the throne of Ardašīr I (224 A.D.) to Xusraw II (590/591-628 A.D.). Consequently, some coins are missing, in particular those concerning the last Sasanian king, Yazdgird III (632-651 A.D.). However, there

[1] I would like to thank several people whose help made possible the publication of this English and Persian edition of the book *La monetazione sasanide nelle Civiche Raccolte Numismatiche di Milano*, Milano 2003. In particular, I would like to thank Prof. Touraj Daryaee (University of California, Irvine), for giving me the opportunity to publish this revised edition and for reading the manuscript, Prof. Antonio Panaino (University of Bologna) for his suggestions, and Prof. Gherardo Gnoli (University of Rome), and Dr. Donatella Caporusso (Conservatore Responsabile delle Civiche Raccolte Archeologiche e Numismatiche di Milano) for encouraging the work; a special thank you also to Mariangela Reina, in relation to the translation of the Italian text, and to Prof. Dr. Michael Alram (Münzkabinett of Wien), Dr. Nikolaus Schindel (ÖAW, Wien) and Prof. Pierfrancesco Callieri (University of Bologna), for their stimulating remarks.

1

are two post-Sasanian coins attributed to the first period of the Arab domination in Iran. These coins, defined as Arab-Sasanian coins by the modern numismatic literature,[2] are one drachm of the governor of Fārs, al-Muhallab ibn Abī Sufrā (694-698 A.D.; Cat. n. 67), and a half-drachm of the Abbasid caliph of Tabaristān, 'Umar ibn al-'Alā (771-780 A.D.; Cat. n. 68).

With this Milanese collection you are given the possibility of going through a five-century period through an artistic and numismatic route. Taking into consideration the exiguous number of pieces collected, it can be supposed that the coins were gathered with the purpose of possessing a simple typological repertory of the Sasanian coins. In fact, it has to be considered that the Arab-

---

[2] Gaube 1973; Gyselen 1984; Gyselen 2000b. The Belgian scholar has focused on the Arab-Sasanian copper coinage, that has been quite neglected up to now; but we should take into consideration that most of the coins under this category are silver drachms and half-drachms, that still present problems of interpretation. The Arab-Sasanian coins are very important because they are a primary source that allows us to follow the intricate events of that period until the end of the Sasanian empire. In fact, since the spread of the Arabs into Iran was gradual (starting from the victory of al-Qādisiyya in 635/636 A.D. and of Nihavand in 641/642 A.D.), the study of the mints allows us to go through the military movements and the progress in conquering the country, even if with many difficulties, due to the "congealment" of the Sasanian coin-types by the Arabs is not always easy to recognize (Nikitin – Roth 1995a). The Arab-Sasanian coins are generally dated either according to the regnal year of the last Sasanian king, Yazdgird III, so the first year corresponds to 632 A.D., or according to a chronology that starts from the death of Yazdgird III, which occurred in 651 A.D., therefore the first year corresponds to 652 A.D., in accordance with such post-Yazdgird calendar (Cat. n. 68). But the Arabs had their own era, the hegira (*Hiğra*), very commonly used also on the coins (Cat. n. 67), that starts with the flight that Muhammad took from Makka to Madina in 622 A.D. The dates on the Arab-Sasanian coins are engraved on the reverse on the left of the altar, fully in continuity with the Sasanian tradition. About the different eras on Arab-Sasanian coins, see: Gyselen 2000b, pp. 86-91.

Sasanian coins can be easily confused with Sasanian issues, since they maintained the iconographic models properly Sasanian[3] for almost two centuries.

Reading the labels along with the coins in the Coin Cabinet, it is evident that a first nucleus of the collection is antique and can be dated to the first half of the nineteenth century (with the inventory number of the Brera collection), whereas a group of thirteen coins was part of a private collection belonging to engineer F. Rolla which was given to the Cabinet during the eighties of the last century. Moreover, from the labels it can also be deducted that the coins were bought one by one from the antiquarian market in Milan during a twenty-year span (seventies and eighties). The most significant nucleus of the collection, such as the Brera coins, was probably bought by order of Gaetano Cattaneo, the eminent founder of the *Medagliere Civico*, for his personal interest in the Arab coins.[4] It has to be re-

---

[3] Although the caliph Abd-al-Malek, governor of Iraq, had reformed the coinage in 698 A.D. (78 H.) introducing coins with inscriptions in Arabic instead of in Pahlavi and without figures but simply epigraphic, some Eastern mints, in part out of the control of the Arabs, such as Samarkand, Bukhara, and Kabul, continued to issue coins with Sasanian iconographies even after the conquest of these regions by the 'Abbāsids, during the second half of the eighth century. See Album, Bates, & Floor, 1993, in particular pp. 17-20; about the reform of the caliph, see Grierson 1960, pp. 241-264.

[4] The Civic Coin Cabinet of Milan was desired and founded by Gaetano Cattaneo (1771-1841), not to be confused with his contemporary Carlo Cattaneo, who was a famous protagonist of the Italian Risorgimento. Gaetano Cattaneo did his best to stop the melting of the coins with some numismatic interest carried out by the mint of Milan, and so some significant pieces were then put in stock beginning in 1803. Eugene de Beauharnais, viceroy of Italy, signed a decree which at last officially founded the Cabinet of coins and medals, in 1808, and Cattaneo was named its first keeper. Thanks to some considerable donations the Coin Cabinet increased its capacity very quickly and it soon became one of the most important Cabinets in Europe, after Paris and Vienna. One of

membered that by that time, under the generic denomination of "Arab coins" the Sasanian coins could easily be included. The two above mentioned Arab-Sasanian coins are part of the nucleus of Brera, whereas a forgery of Ardašīr I (Cat. n. 69) is certainly a nineteenth century cast piece which also shows antiquarian interest for these types of non-classic coins.[5]

---

the numismatic enterprises carried out by Cattaneo (who was also a good painter, and a bibliophile esteemed by Alessandro Manzoni, but a very bad archaeologist), was to obtain a catalogue of a vast collection of Arab-Islamic coins purchased at the Museum of Dresden. The catalogue, drawn up by the Orientalist C. Castiglioni, with the preface written by Cattaneo himself, was ready in 1819, with the title: *Catalogo delle monete Cufiche dell'I.R. Museo di Milano.* Cattaneo even induced the State property office to buy the Arabic printing characters which, at that time, could not be found in all of Milan. Unfortunately, the catalogue encountered very little success both with the critics, not benevolent with him at all, and the public. Perhaps Cattaneo was ahead of his time with this publication concerning Oriental coins that in Italy turned out to be of no interest. So Cattaneo was frustrated not only because of the disappointing results of the publication of the catalogue, but also because it was very difficult to deal with the administration of the Austrian invaders. In a letter he wrote in 1811 it can be read: – *Dio sa che mai vi troveranno gli accigliati aristarchi coi loro acutissimi microscopi, nelle lenti dei quali non v'è particella che rifranga neppure un sol raggio sulle parti commendevoli delle opere che prendono in esame* – "only God knows what the severe critics can find by their elaborated microscopes, in which lens no one particle refracts not even one ray on the literary works worthy of praise that they take under examination." My hypothesis is that the Sasanian coins involved, such as the coins of the Brera's collection, perhaps come from the same lot purchased in Dresden in 1812. Obviously, this hypothesis should be supported by archival data that unfortunately, in this case, is either not in existence or very difficult to find. On the history of the Coin Cabinet in Milan, see La Guardia 1985 and Savio & Della Ferrara 1990.

[5] The only scholar who has carried out studies on the modern Sasanian counterfeits, trying to individualize some different workshops is Robert Göbl. He is also the founder of Sasanian numismatics. See Göbl 1954 and Göbl 1971, pp. 59-62, pl. 16.

For what concerns the filing of the material, I have followed the criteria used in the modern texts of Göbl (1971), Alram & Gyselen (2003) and Schindel (2004). The first line in bold refers to the transliteration of the legend in Middle-Persian[6] that can be found on the coin; the second line offers the phonetic transcription. This sequence proved to be useful and necessary as various Middle-Iranian languages not only utilized a writing system of Aramaic origin, but also can be identified for the wide use of heterograms or logograms, such as real Aramaic forms which were contextually read according to the local language such as Middle-Persian, Parthian, or other forms.[7] As per convention, such heterograms are always transliterated in capital letters but they can also be followed by lower-case letters used for Iranian grammatical complements.

I hope that this catalogue of the Sasanian coins preserved at the *Medagliere* in Milan will be of stimulus for the publication of Sasanian coins of other Coin Cabinets throughout Italy.[8] In the last few years in fact, the Viennese

---

[6] Middle-Persian is mostly used on coins and on royal inscriptions, but is also found on seals, *cretulae*, parchments, *ostraca* and papyri. It has to be noted that Middle-Persian is an Iranian language, as well as the Parthian, the Sogdian, the Choresmian and the Bactrian. These languages use the heterographic system with peculiar developments according to each tradition. The Middle-Iranian period is nearly included between the end of the Achaemenid Empire (fourth century B.C.) and the tenth century A.D., although Middle-Iranian languages were still used, especially in Outer-Iran and in Central Asia until the twelfth and thirteenth centuries (Cereti 2001, pp. 13-21).

[7] An exemplary case is the inscriptional Middle-Persian or Pahlavi *šāhān šāh*, "King of Kings," that in Middle-Persian is written MLKAn MLKA, which instead in Parthian it is written MLKYN MLKA. To be noted the Middle-Persian plural ending in –*ān*, indicated as *n* in MLKA*n*. I have followed MacKenzie 1971 for the transliteration of the Middle-Persian on the coins.

[8] Some Sasanian coins, preserved at the History and Art Museum of Trieste, have been published by Bravar 1982; a few Parthian and Sa-

and French Schools, in collaboration with the "Istituto Italiano per l'Africa e l'Oriente (IsIAO)" of Rome, have planned to achieve a *Sylloge Nummorum Sasanidarum* (SNS), and let us hope that the present work will be of some contribution.

1.2 Coinage and art of the Sasanians through the analysis of their crowns.

The accession to the throne of the Sasanian dynasty[9] begins with the rebellion of Ardašīr I against the Parthian king Artabanos IV (213-224 A.D.), who was finally defeated in the battle of Hormizdagān. Within a few years the Sasanians succeeded in taking possession of most of the Parthian empire and they then settled down in the capital, Ctesiphon, moving from the little region of Persis (situated in the South-West of Iran which was the political and religious heart of the dynasty). The Sasanians take their name from Sāsān, who was the chief priest at the important sanctuary of the goddess Anāhitā[10] in Staxr, the capital of the Persis region (present Fārs). Sāsān was an ancestor, perhaps the grandfather of Ardašīr, son of Pābag, but there

---

sanian coins are also preserved in the Coin Cabinet of Bologna, see Gariboldi 2004b.

[9] For a history of the Sasanian empire, see Christensen 1944; Frye 1984; Schippmann 1990; Morony 1995; and more recently Wiesehöfer 2001, with an exhaustive bibliography.

[10] Anāhitā (M.P. Anāhīd) is the great goddess of water and her name means "immaculate," but she was also invoked as goddess for fertility and procreation, even if a warlike temper was attributed to her. She was widely worshipped, along with Ohrmazd and Mithra (M.P. Mihr), during the entire Sasanian period, particularly in Persis (Gray 1929). She is represented on some Sasanian rock reliefs in the act of crowning the king (Gyselen 2000a, p. 303), and this scene is probably represented also on Wahrām II's coins, see Cat. n. 8. About the story of Sāsān and the Greek sources, see Gariboldi 2005.

are different and mythical stories about him. These princes took profit of the inheritance of the Achaemenids[11] monuments of whom were still well visible in Pasargadae and in Persepolis on their territory.

Deducing from the coinage, the kings of Persis had always benefited from a condition of partial autonomy, as compared to the Parthians. In fact, on the coins (first coinage around 200-180 B.C.) they used the Aramaic language instead of Greek.[12] On the obverse they display the bust of

---

[11] Daryaee 2002a.

[12] Starting from the Achaemenid period, the Aramaic was used in a vast area, as the texts written in such a language could circulate easier than the cuneiform tablets. Therefore, different Iranian languages, such as Parthian or Middle-Persian, are based on a writing system mainly coming from Aramaic, however with the addition of many words written in Aramaic but pronounced in the corresponding Iranian phonetic form (heterograms or logograms). This arameographic writing system implies a long period during which Aramaic had to be a supporting language, commonly used in the administrative chancelleries where the scribes were in charge of the translation of Aramaic texts in various Iranian languages and vice versa. As far as the numismatic material is concerned, it has to be remembered that even if, on the one hand, it is ascertained that the Parthians mainly used the Greek language for commercial and political purposes on their coins (which was not used anymore around the half of the first century A.D.; then the inscriptions looked like a kind of pseudo-legend in Greek that probably even the engravers could not understand), on the other hand, Aramaic legends can be found on some coins of Arsaces I. In fact, in the hoard (about 2,000 coins) found in the valley of the Atrek river near Bujnūrd, in the North-East of Iran, there are some drachms attributed to Arsaces I (around 220-215 B.C.), with inscriptions in Greek and Aramaic, which were probably struck at Nisa. The Greek word *autokratoros,* which was engraved on the first emissions, sometimes appears *krny* which is perhaps related to the mighty Parthian family of the Kārēn, but that nevertheless was equivalent to the term *strategos* in the Achaemenid use and therefore semantically similar to *autokrator.* On this matter, see Abgarians & Sellwood 1971; Sellwood 1983, pp. 279-281, pl. I, 2: Wolski 1993, pp. 69-70. The publication of this hoard has been of extreme importance for numismatic studies as it testifies not only to the use of

their kings who are very often given high-sounding names which come from the typical onomatology of the Achaemenids, such as Dārā (Darius) or Ardašīr (Artaxerxes). On the reverse they use the iconography of the ever-burning fire altar with the king standing beside it in homage to the god Ahura Mazdā, the veneration of whom was likely higher during the Achaemenid period than during the Parthian era. The Parthians, in fact, showed religious syncretism with the Greek divinities and even declared on some coins to be "friends of the Greeks," not just for supine philhellenism, it seems to me, but for sharing a political realism focused on the ethnical integration of the Greek population.[13]

It is no surprise at all that the Sasanians used on the coins a similar iconography without changing it for almost four centuries. It is my opinion that the close relation between the Fratarakas[14] and the Sasanians, their descen-

---

Aramaic starting from the origin of the Arsacid dynasty, therefore with a differentiation from the Seleucid dynasty, but especially because it allows attribution of the first Parthian coins to Arsaces I and Arsaces II, instead of Mithridates I, as it was claimed in the past, for example, by Göbl 1978, I, p. 94. These sources testify to a sort of Neo-Iranism starting from the early Parthian period: see Wolski 1993.

[13] Mithridates I started to put on his coins the title ΦΙΛΕΛΛΕΝΟΣ, and then many other Parthian kings did the same. See Head 1911, p. 819; Sellwood 1983, pp. 282-298. He was also the first to declare himself King of Kings of the Parthians, but this title was not engraved on the coins. The legend βασιλευς βασιλέων appears only starting from Mithridates II (123-87 B.C.). See Sellwood 1983, p. 285, pl. II, 10; Wolski 1993, pp. 97-99.

[14] The pre-Sasanian kings of Persis are indicated with this name, as when on the coins it is written *pltlk'* – precisely *frataraka* (Alram 1986, pp. 162-186). An old reading of the word *fratadora* leads to the translation "fire keepers" but with the finding of an Aramaic papyrus from Egypt on which is written the term *prtrk*, referring to an Achaemenid officer of a lower position than satrap, but in any case important, allows us to translate at last the term *frataraka* on the coins with "governor,"

dants, has not yet been underlined sufficiently, at least for what concerns the coin iconography with the ideological implications. A rare type of coin,[15] probably issued in Persis between 205/206 (the year in which the Sasanians began their domain – maybe the same year of the accession of Pābag?) and 224 A.D., when the real Sasanian coinage began in the name of Ardašīr, shows on the obverse Ardašīr in frontal view, in accordance with an iconographic scheme deduced from the Parthians,[16] and, on the reverse,

---

"prefect" (Panaino 2003a, p. 265, note 1). It is to be noted that the legend on the coins of the first Fratarakas, is *frataraka ī bayān*, probably meaning "the governor (for the sake/in the name) of the gods." The gods referred to were likely the gods of the old Mazdean religion, worshipped by the Achaemenids (Panaino 2003a, pp. 283-284); another possibility is that the *bayān* were the deceased Achaemenid kings (Callieri 1998, p. 36).

[15] Alram & Gyselen 2003, Typ. I/1.

[16] The first Parthian coin on which the king is frontally represented should probably be attributed to Darius (?) (70 B.C.). This iconographic typology appears again with Artabanos II (10/11-38 A.D.), Vonones II (43/44-51 A.D.), Vologeses V (191/192-207/208 A.D.), see Sellwood 1983. Also, some Sasanian kings are represented in this posture, usually on celebrative gold coins, such as Wahrām IV, Kawād I, Xusraw I, and Xusraw II. However, Xusraw II is also represented in frontal view on some rare silver drachms (Göbl 1971, pl. 14, ns. 218-219), where on the reverse is represented another frontal bust with the head surrounded by flames, perhaps the representation of the *xwarrah* (the Splendour, the vital strength infused by Ohrmazd, who grants the sacred royalty to the sovereign), according to Gyselen 2000a. It can be assumed that the frontal representation for the Sasanian kings was a regal posture that was assumed in royal representations only under particular circumstances when they clearly wanted to show evidence of the close and privileged relationship between the king and the god, the latter being the source of kingship. In this way, the heroic and divine aspect of the king was emphasized. In fact, on the Sasanian seals both the divinities and the heroes are frontally represented. Further proof confirming that it is actually royalty being emphasized by this extraordinary iconography is the additional legend "King of Kings" that Xusraw II engraved on this special emission, considering that normally his coins did not have this title anymore. Moreover, it cannot be excluded that the Sa-

the bust of Pābag turned left, who wears a regal tiara of
Parthian style,[17] such as a high and circular calotte, with

---

sanian propaganda of Xusraw II had as ideological external referent the
Byzantine Empire, ruled by Heraclius (610-641 A.D.), as during his
reign the fight against the Sasanians became more violent and dramatic.
It is sufficient to remember the conquest of Jerusalem by the Persians in
614 A.D. (the Holy Cross was removed and taken to Ctesiphon), and the
consequent renewal of hostilities by the Byzantines. The frontal position
of the sovereign, clearly of Oriental origin, was introduced in the West
in the third century A.D., and appeared for the first time on rare gold
coins (noble metal was preferred) of the Roman emperor Postumus
(259-268 A.D.), and then exceptionally adopted by Maxentius, Licinius
II and Constantine I. Soon it became common in Roman imperial art.
See Bastien 1992-1994; Vermeule 1956-1957.

[17] Concerning the Parthian crowns also represented on coins of Ardašīr I
and of the Fratarakas, see Peck 1993. The coming of the Arsacids
(around 250 B.C.) as, in a certain way, they were influenced by the
Greek tradition (this is mainly due both to the prestige exerted by Greek
culture and to the rather high number of people of Greek origin present
in the Parthian reign), led to the restoring of the use of the Greek diadem that was slightly modified during the centuries ahead. Also, the
Greek term for diadem (διάδημα) entered the Iranian languages (in the
Parthian and Middle-Persian inscriptions we have *dydymy*, in Pahlavi
dēhēm). So, for example, Mithridates III (58-53 B.C.) doubled it and wore
it with long ribbons, while the last Parthian kings wore multiple sashes
tied with short ribbons and placed them on cluster-styled hair, antici-
pating in this way the Sasanian hair style. For a certain period, a hat
with soft top (*kyrbasia*) was also used, different from the so-called
Phrygian hat, with the ear protection tied under the chin and encircled
by the diadem (for example, on the first issues of Mithridates I, 171-138
B.C.). This kind of cap was already used by Persian nomads and it was
only the diadem that conferred royal dignity. But besides the use of the
diadem, what has to be considered is the important introduction of the
real and proper crown by Mithridates II king of the Parthians (123-87
B.C.), called mitre or tiara (it is represented on the coins around 100
B.C.: see Wroth 1903, p. 76, pl. VIII/1-2). It is a high and circular hat with
ear and nape protections, decorated with a dotted line and star and
usually had a diadem. Mithridates II was the first king of the Parthians
to be defined on the coins as King of kings, and the decision to use a
new hat, substantially different from the simple Greek diadem (the
white band used by the Seleucids), seems to be in relation with a precise

ear flaps and nape-guard adorned with diadem and dotted all along its borders. A regal symbol is in the centre distinguishing the Iranian noble families: in this case it is a lunar crescent surrounding a little disk. This issue was struck during the first minting phase of Ardašīr, when he was just known as *bay Ardašīr šāh* (Lord Ardašīr King), and not yet *šāhān šāh*.

The close bond between the dynasts of the post-Achaemenid Fārs and Ardašīr, who was just the last of the Fratarakas and the first king of the Sasanians, can also be noticed in considering the development of the crowns. In fact, Göbl was able to check six different kinds of crowns worn by Ardašīr (type VII is a hybrid). The first (type I/1 of Fig. 2: from Göbl 1971, table 1-1a) follows the tradition of the crowns of the Fratarakas, with a crescent in the centre and a disk. This crown is inherent to the period in which Ardašīr was a local ruler and when he and his young brother Šābuhr, had to face internal dynastic struggles, but with the early accidental death of Šābuhr, Ardašīr had no rivals at all.

The second crown (type II of Fig. 2) is quite similar to the mitre-crown of Mithridates II king of the Parthians, and also similar to the caps of the Fratarakas, and probably goes back to the period of the victory over Artabanos IV, from whom in a certain way the crown was usurped. However, the decorations of the mitre can change; most of the time there are stars and there are also circles or a kind of triskelion and the *frawahr*, the symbol of the royal investiture, such as a ring with long ribbons (type II/2b).

---

political choice to hold on to the old Iranian tradition. The regal mitre was sometimes adorned with crests or different symbols, such as horns, deer heads or anchors (perhaps the heraldic insignia of the most important Parthian families), and it remained the most original and characteristic Parthian crown. See Piras 2000, pp. 15-19; Gariboldi 2000, pp. 55-56, note 17.

The third crown (type III. Cat. ns. 1-2) is the most important one since, for the first time, the high *korymbos* is represented on the cap and this will characterize the real and typical crowns of the Sasanians. The hair is divided in two parts: along the neck and the sides of the head, several curly long plaits are coming out from a dotted calotte; on the top of the head there is a big tuft which is globe shaped, fastened by a veil, perhaps made of silk and always dotted.[18] The long ribbons of the diadem, placed on the forehead, are fluttering behind the head and other two little sashes tie the globe on the calotte. Starting from Pērōz and Kawād I (Cat. ns. 33-36; 39-41), these ribbons are going to be symmetrically placed behind the king's shoulders and turned upwards, one on the left and the other one on the right, with few exceptions.[19] The purpose of these variations seems to be both the attempt to introduce a differentiation compared with the iconography of the previous kings and in general, rather extraneous to the whole Iranian art.

In addition to all these aspects, we cannot forget how important the colours of the crowns were, such as, green, red, blue, and white, and the way they were matched dif-

---

[18] Göbl 1971, pp. 7-8; Peck 1993, pp. 413-414.

[19] Walaxš (484-488 A.D.) replaced the right ribbon with a flame on his shoulder (Cat. ns. 37-38). The meaning of this flame is not clear, even if the role of fire and light (*xwarrah*) is of primary importance in the Zoroastrian religion. However, the flame on the shoulder may come from a Central-Asiatic tradition, considering that it was used by the kings of the Kušān Empire and in the art of the Gandhāra (Göbl 1971, page 15). Concerning the chronology of the Kušāns, about the art and coinage of this important Iranian empire that developed from the first to the fourth century A.D., see: Alram & Klimburg Salter 1999; Errington, Sarkhosh & Curtis 2007. Zāmāsp (496-499 A.D.) is represented on the coins, instead of the right ribbon, a small bust, probably of Ohrmazd, in the act of handing the royal diadem of the investiture (Göbl 1971, pl. 11, ns. 180-181; Schindel 2004, 3/1, pp. 450-451).

ferently. The Muslim historian Mas'ūdī (tenth century A.D.), for example, says that the crown of Ardašīr was green on gold, and that of Yazdgird III was bright red.[20] The tradition to use different colours for the crowns with different meanings is oriental and started in ancient times. An example is the combination of the Pharaonic ceremonial of the red (Lower Egypt) and white crown (Upper Egypt) and when they were put together it meant the union of the two domains. When they were represented separately, it meant the North and the South of Egypt. Moreover, during the Byzantine age the sovereigns always came back to the palace wearing the white crown because the palace was settled at the South in respect to the other buildings, and the remaining colours were used in accordance to the other festivities (Const. Porphyr. *De caer.* I 46, 37).

The other typologies of the crowns of Ardašīr allude, according to Göbl, to divine investitures and, therefore, are to be considered "special" crowns. So the crown type IV with merlons, used also by the Achaemenid kings,[21] of far away Mesopotamian origin, should refer to Ahura Mazdā (M.P. Ohrmazd), who is represented on Sasanian rock reliefs wearing this type of crown. In fact, a relief of Naqš-i Rustam (Fig. 3),[22] religious and funerary centre of the Achaemenids, whose protection the Sasanians seemed to

---

[20] Mas'ūdī, *Kitāb al-tanbīh*, pp.150-151; Erdmann 1951; Carile 2000, pp. 82, 115-116, note 26.

[21] Peck 1993, p. 407.

[22] Alram 2000, p. 268, Abb. 9; Ghirshman 1962, pp. 131-132. Another relief at Firuzabad shows Ohrmazd handing the crown to Ardašīr, but here the two figures are standing on the sides of a little altar and behind them there is a retinue of three men, perhaps the king's sons and a page-boy.

ask, shows a mighty scene of a horseback investiture of ancient Iranian tradition between Ohrmazd and Ardašīr.[23]

Obviously the investiture is represented ideologically but we have to recall that, as it happened, the Sasanians used to crown themselves until Wahrām V (420-438 A.D.) introduced the custom of being crowned by the Great Priest (*mowbedān mowbed*) at the moment of the solemn investiture. In this way, the political power of the king was ratified by the religious authority of the Magi. The patriarch of Constantinople followed this usage, perhaps a case of imitation between the two great powers, starting from 491 A.D., when he had to crown the Roman emperor.[24]

On the relief Ohrmazd and Ardašīr are represented in heraldic position, facing each other, and the god offers with the right hand a "big diadem" (M.P. *wuzurg dēhēm*), with long ribbons, to the king, who receives it with the stretched arm while rising the left hand with the bent forefinger, as a gesture of deference. Usually this behaviour was typical of people of lower rank when they were in front of the king.

Ohrmazd wears a crown with merlons and holds with the left hand the *barsom*, a bundle of sacred twigs. Ardašīr wears the crown with the great *korymbos* (type III of the coins) that is even higher than the crown of the god and on

---

[23] This is testified by the inscriptions in Middle-Persian engraved under the two figures. The first inscription says: "this is the representation of Ohrmazd the God" (M.P.: *paykar ēn Ohrmazd-bay*), and the second one: "this is the representation of the Mazdean Lord Ardašīr, King of Kings" (M.P.: *paykar ēn māzdēsn bay Ardašīr šāhān šāh*). Note that the term *bay*, when placed after the name of the divinity, means "God", while when preceding the king's name, as engraved on the coins, means "Lord". These linguistic peculiarities are important in understanding the spirit of the Sasanian kingship, for which the king, although "divine" in relation with his subjects, cannot be considered a real god like a Mazdean divinity (*yazd*). See Panaino 2003a, pp. 275-276.

[24] Nöldeke 1879, p. 96; Shahbazi 1993, p. 278.

which anthropomorphism is evident. Both of them wear long dresses but the pleats of the drapery have a heavy metallic aspect so they do not transmit any sense of movement. The mighty horses, however, are too tiny in respect to the gigantic horsemen. Behind Ardašīr there is a page who wears a hat of mitre shape, but not decorated, and who holds a fly-flap. Under the hooves of the horses are the enemies defeated by both of them: on the left side is the head of Artabanos crushed on the ground (who still wears the regal mitre); on the right side there is the horrible head of Ahreman,[25] the evil god beaten by Ohrmazd. This representation is strongly symbolic and in just one picture admirably gathers the theme of the divine investiture and the royal victory. The first ratifies the second and launches the message of the fusion and of the close dependence on politics and religion between the supreme god and the king. Ardašīr, who receives directly from Ohrmazd the power, defeats his enemies in a real war that has its cosmic-universal antithesis in the everlasting fight between Good and Evil, but where is expected a final triumph of the positive forces that are enlightened by the glory of Ohrmazd.

The crown of the king is extremely important, since it gives the expression of the *xwarrah*, the divine splendour that is the source of energy, victory, fortune and knowl-

---

[25] Ahreman, in opposition to Ohrmazd, represents the Evil One in the strongly dualistic Mazdean religious system. He, "dull to reach the knowledge," lives in the dark abyss, "he was, he is and however he will not be" (*Bundahišn* 1, 2), whereas Ohrmazd "he was, he is, and he will be for ever" (*būd ud ast ud hamē bawēd*), because he will capture and annihilate the malign spirit, confining him into the "historic time", from which Ahreman will not be able to get out anymore. Ahreman looses his battle also at a universal and meta-temporal level (Zaehner 1955, pp. 287, 312). In the late Pahlavi texts, the name of Ahreman is usually written upside-down.

edge. If the *xwarrah* abandons the privileged man, in the event he commits a sin, he will become a lost man and will not be able to carry out his mission against Evil. The sovereign who loses the *xwarrah*, loses his royalty and will have a poor destiny. As a matter of fact, the Sasanian kings used to change the crown every time they were badly defeated or the throne was usurped; in this way the *xwarrah* was symbolically restored.[26]

The artist that made this relief has fully achieved his propagandistic aim with a powerful ideological message, one that proposes the new Sasanian political and religious conception based on the foundations of the monarchy and of the Zoroastrian church,[27] in the name of an antique as

---

[26] Gnoli 1991, pp. 115-118; Gnoli 1999, p. 315; underlines the relation between the *xwarrah* and the *Tyche*, the indispensable quality for the sovereign.

[27] About Zoroastrianism, see Zaehner 1955; Gnoli 1991, with critical bibliography, and also Gnoli 2000; Stausberg 2002. I merely note here that Zoroastrianism, founded by the prophet Zoroaster, perhaps existed in Eastern Iran between the tenth to seventh century B.C., and was probably the religion of the Achaemenid dynasty up to the disastrous coming of the "accursed" (M.P. *gizistag*) Alexander the Great who supposedly set fire to the *Avesta* and destroyed the caste of the Magi, as well as many believers. After surviving to the Parthian and the Seleucid period, characterized by the spreading of Greek divinities, Zoroastrianism, or Mazdeism, from the name of Ahura Mazdā, the "Wise Lord", became the official religion of the new Sasanian empire under which a powerful Zoroastrian church was organized (at present there still are minor Zoroastrian communities in Iran and India), framed in a rigid hierarchy of *mowbed*s and *hērbed*s, priests and doctors in religion, who could also hold some civil and administrative offices (Gyselen 1989a; 2002). During the Sasanian period, the official written codification of the *Avesta* was carried out. The essential feature of Zoroastrianism is the worship of a unique supreme god and creator, the omniscient, Ahura Mazdā, who stands at the top of a hierarchy of divine entities, the implacable antagonist of the prince of darkness, Ahreman. The fight between Good and Evil is conducted without exclusion of any stroke, both concerning

well as religious tradition that gives a new strong national identity to the whole of Iran.[28] To linger over the lack of naturalism, of muscularity and on the gravity of the figures, does not grant any merit to this kind of art that strives to be symbolic and timeless. Even the sculptures of this period display a strong plasticity; a more elevated and projecting relief compared, for example, to the Parthian rock relief, undoubtedly flattering.[29]

The type V (Fig. 2) of Ardašīr's crown is a particular one, as the hair is styled with the *korymbos* as it used to be, but without any dotted veils, and therefore visible are the long plaits knotted behind the back and on the head in order to get a big waving tuft. The hair on the forehead is held by the diadem with long and elaborated ribbons, the ends of which were probably tied with coloured sashes.

This hair style can be seen only on a few coins[30] and is also visible on a large rock relief (Fig. 4) that stands out in a mountain gorge leading to the city of Firuzabad [31] which was built by Ardašīr as his capital and named *Ardašīr-xwarrah* (Ardašīr's Glory). Perhaps even during this period

---

the moral and ritual sphere, carried out in a deep, ontological, ethical, and total metaphysical dualism.

[28] Zoroastrianism assumed the characteristics of a national faith linked with the idea of Iran; an idea that sprang out thanks to the Sasanian propaganda beginning in the third century A.D. The Iranian kings were so conscious both of their national identity and of the authority they exerted on non-Iranian people, that they added to their official titles *šāhān šāh Ērān ud anērān*, "King of Kings of the Iranians and non-Iranians", starting with Šābuhr I, but this addition was not included on his coins. This title is engraved on the coins starting with Ohrmazd I (272-273 A.D.). It is strong nationalism that insists on the ethnicity of the Aryans, that goes beyond a local dimension and that is, anyhow, not denied. On this subject see Gnoli 1971, Gnoli 1989 and Gnoli 1998.

[29] Ghirshman 1962, pp. 52-56.

[30] Göbl, 1971, pl. 1, n.16.

[31] At Firuzabad there is also the fortress of Ardašīr at the top of an inaccessible rocky peak (Genito 2001).

he was preparing the rebellion against the Parthians. This relief, perhaps the most ancient of Sasanian art, is long (almost twenty metres) and is a triptych: it represents the mounted soldier battles symbolizing all the victories on the enemies in a hierarchical and paratactic order. Ardašīr on a war-horse spurred in a "flying gallop" hits and, with a long lance, unsaddles Artabanos, who looks like a defenceless puppet. Behind Ardašīr is his successor son who kills Darbendān, the Grand Vizier of the Parthian king, and moreover, there is a Sasanian cavalryman who grabs at the neck of an enemy.

Due to its poor projection and the style of near and matching figures, this relief, under the artistic point of view, is almost equal to those made by the Parthians without any indication of landscape or time, whereas the scene, although dramatic, has been steadily engraved in the rock. It is quite evident that we are far away from the Roman relief and any kind of comparison seems to be useless, even if the symbolic and propagandistic final effect is as strong. Yet, the divine intervention is missing and was instead represented in the relief of Naqš-i Rustam which should be likely set in a more mature period of Sasanian art and ideology. On the other hand, it can be noted on the relief of Firuzabad a very accurate attention for the decorative details, which are typical of subsequent Sasanian art. As an example, the caparisons of the horses as well as the quivers are quilted with tens of regal symbols and the manes are styled in a globe shape and tied with ribbons, as are the tails, in accordance with the elaborate style used for regal hair. Ardašīr and his retinue wear heavy cataphracts, whereas the Parthians here did not. The king wears the characteristic necklace of pearls and a big disk on his chest that is kept in central position by crossed sashes (like the *kardiophylax* of the Greek panoplies), and a ring into which his beard is retained. All *regalia* can also be seen on the coins.

The type VI of the crown (Fig. 2) can be referred again to a divine investiture, in this case concerning Anāhitā, to whom was dedicated the important temple of Staxr, of which Ardašīr was the Great priest, according to the ancestral tradition. As a matter of fact, the crown has a mitre shape and is equipped with cheek protections and is decorated with an image of an eagle with open wings holding a ribbon in its beak. The eagle recalls Anāhitā, but this crown can be seen on coins only.

Consequently, the coins of Ardašīr I allow us to go through the development of his crowns, from those of Parthian style (used also by the Fratarakas) to those of proper Sasanian shape that are also represented on the reliefs.

It is peculiar to note that the king's crown with the nape-guard and cheek protections is not represented on the famous reliefs that celebrate the victories of Šābuhr I (240-272 A.D.) over the Romans[32] (Fig. 5), during a series of military campaigns the chronology of which is yet under the study by historians.[33] This type of crown instead, appears on most of his coins (Cat. ns. 3-7). Šābuhr had even ordered to cut at Fārs five reliefs with the purpose to

---

[32] Ghirshman 1962, pp. 151-161. See also Alram 2000, p. 271

[33] Gordianus III attacked the Persians but he died in the battle of Misikhē in 244 A.D. and consequently Philippus the Arab surrendered, paying an onerous tribute of money in order to ransom himself and his troops. According to the inscription of Šābuhr (Huyse 1999: I, p. 27; II, pp. 51-52), Philippus had to give to the Persians 500,000 *dēnārs* (*dynr* IIIIIC), certainly in gold (see also Alram & Gyselen 2003, p. 164). Finally, during a third catastrophic campaign for the Romans, the emperor Valerianus was captured near Edessa by Šābuhr in 260 A.D. and this victory was greatly emphasised by Sasanian propaganda. The Roman sources, on the contrary, are rather reticent about these events. See Gnoli T. 2000, pp. 146-153.

propagandize and celebrate his victories which had heavy casualties for the Roman army. These events do not appear on the coins, as far as we know, since on the reverse of them is represented the sacred fire altar flanked by two attendants. For what concerns the victories, we can find a detailed description in the great trilingual inscription of Šābuhr on the *Ka'ba-i Zardušt*,[34] wrote in Middle-Persian, Parthian and Greek, well-known with the name of *Res Gestae Divi Saporis* (this denomination goes back to Rostovcev). Nowadays, many arguments lead to date it between the capture of the emperor Valerianus (260 A.D.) and the war against Odainat of Palmyra (262 A.D.), so not *post mortem*.[35]

Šābuhr I wears a mural crown, recalling that of Ohrmazd, on top of which is a great *korymbos*. From beneath the crown, along the sides of the face, are thick tufts of curly hair. This is the iconography represented on the reliefs as well as on the statues. I am referring to the colossal statue of Šābuhr that was found in a cave near Bišāpūr (Fig. 6),[36] nearly twenty feet high, with a stylized waved drapery, perhaps made up for funerary purposes. As it happened, the Zoroastrians were not used to burying corpses as they could contaminate earth and water, sacred elements. Therefore, they were laid on the top of the so called "towers of silence" where they were eaten by birds of prey.[37] Afterward, the bones were collected and put into

---

[34] For the inscription and comments, see Huyse 1999.

[35] In the inscription Šābuhr defines himself as *māzdēsn bay* "Mazdean Lord", in accordance with a royal title shown also on the coins. But the term *bay* cannot be compared, without a deeper discussion, with the Latin *divus* (Panaino 2000, p. 23, note 2): About the term *mazdēsn* or **māzdēsn* see Panaino 2003b, and Huyse 1999: II, p. 6, note 17.

[36] Ghirshman 1962, p.165.

[37] Gnoli 1991, p. 117.

cinerary urns. So it is likely that the statue of Šābuhr was conceived as funerary signal.

We have noticed on the coins that the crown worn by Šābuhr is similar but not identical to those represented on the reliefs. As proof that sometimes the artists could elaborate on their own the iconography of the crowns, we can consider the famous cameo in sardonyx preserved in the Bibliothèque Nationale that probably represents the encounter on horseback between Šābuhr and Valerianus (Fig. 7).[38] Valerianus brandishes the sword, while Šābuhr grasps with his right hand the wrist of the Roman without drawing his sword, even though his hand is already placed on the hilt of it. This gesture of the "grasp" of the hand is quite significant as it symbolically means the capture of the enemy. In fact, on four Iranian reliefs Šābuhr grasps the hand or the wrists of Valerianus in accordance with the precise words of his great inscription (ŠKZ 22, 2),[39] written in Middle-Persian, Parthian and Greek:

> MP.: *AP[n] wly['lnwsy kysly] BNPŠE PWN NPŠE YD[E] dstglwby krt[y]*
> Pa.: *W w'lrnyws kysr BNPŠE pty NPŠE YDA dstgrb OBDt*
> Gr.: καί Οὐαλεριανόν Καίσαρα ἡμεις ἐν ἰδίαις χερσίν ἐκρατήσαμεν
> "And we caught (prisoner) in our own hands Valerianus Caesar".

---

[38] This famous cameo is preserved at the Bibliothèque Nationale of Paris. On the cameo, about which divergent opinions are still under discussion, see Göbl 1974 pp. 33-38; Gall 1990, pp. 56-59, has supposed that the cameo represents Šābuhr II with Jovian; Wiesehöfer 2001, p. 163 (Pl. XXVIIb), has advanced the opinion that the cameo could have been created by a Roman artist by order of a later Sasanian king. See now Betti 2008, with further bibliography.

[39] This curious parallelism was noted for the first time by MacDermot 1954, pp. 76-80. For the inscription see Huyse 1999: I, p. 37.

I think that the repetition of this gesture even on the cameo can be considered as an indication of the fact that it was engraved under a strong Sasanian influence. Moreover, the horses are at a "flying gallop", as on the relief of Ardašīr at Firuzabad, and the horse harnesses are of typical Sasanian style, too. On the one hand, we can see that the face of Valerianus does not have any particular features but has, as represented on the reliefs, impersonal and atypical somatic traits, if compared, for example, to the Roman coins of Valerianus; on the other hand, there is the intent to give the impression that he is a Roman man from his clothes and the lack of beard. Only the laurel-crown confirms that he is an emperor. Strangely enough, Šābuhr wears a crown on the top of which there is a high *korymbos*, but without merlons as on the relief at Dārāb. Göbl considered it a lighter crown more suitable for wearing during combat. However, we can see the presence of the cheek protections that are not represented on the reliefs; there is even a ring stringed at the end of the beard and the crossed braces on the chest. The fact that the musculature of Šābuhr is rather marked cannot be taken as a certain proof of the attribution of this artistic object to western workmanship.[40]

In the event Sasanians asked for the cooperation of western skilled workers in order to carry out this glyptic work of art (one of the Roman prisoners deported to Iran?) would testify once again to the symbolic spirit of Iranian art and it is likely that the Persians at least had to supply a model to the engraver of the cameo, which was not a material commonly used in Sasanian glyptic.

Following Šābuhr, other kings, in order to be recognized, adopted elements which appeared on the crowns of the gods in addition to the *korymbos* that was always pres-

---

[40] Shepherd 1983, pp. 1100-1101.

ent. For example, the rayed crown of Wahrām I (273-276 A.D.) refers to Mithra, while the winged crown of Wahrām II (276-293 A.D.) alludes to Vərəθraγna (M.P. Wahrām), god of the victorious assault in Iranian mythology, represented by an eagle, a boar or a horse, and also by a heroic young man (see *Wahrām Yašt*, or *Yašt* 14). On the coin n. 8 of our Catalogue, Wahrām wears the winged crown on the top of which there is a large *korymbos*, while his wife Šābuhrduxtag,[41] whose bust is represented near her hus-

---

[41] The confirmation that the personage involved is indeed the queen comes from either the iconographic confrontation with reliefs or from a coin on which there is the legend *šhypwhrdwhtky* MLKT'*n* MLKT', "Šābuhrduxtag Queen of Queens" (Choksy 1989, pp. 122-123), not known to Göbl 1971, since he writes on p. 54: "whose name (Wahrām II's wife) we do not know". Moreover, her name appears also on the great inscription of Šābuhr I, as she was the daughter of Šābuhr king of Mesene (l.21). The title of MLKT'*n* MLKT (MP. and Parthian *bāmbišnān bāmbišn*, Greek βασίλισσα των βασιλισσων) is also used in the inscription for Dēnag, sister and wife of Ardašīr I (1. 23) and for Āduranāhīd, daughter and wife (Huyse 1999: II, p. 107) of Šābuhr I (1. 18). Marriages between blood-relations (M.P. *xwēdōdah*) were normally celebrated among the Zoroastrians and, obviously, they were more frequent in the regal circle. The use of representing the portrait of a queen on coins is of Hellenistic origin and it started just after the introduction of the physiognomic portrait in the Greek coinage, widely spread during and after the period of Alexander the Great. The idea of representing the portrait of a live queen is probably attributed to Lysimachus, and to the new cultural trend developed inside the institutional and political contexts of the Hellenistic kingdoms. It is interesting to me to note what Aristotle writes in *Polit.* II, 1269b, 20-25, about the power of women. According to him, this power is more like a *gynaikokratia*, rather than a real *basileia* (in fact, in the autocratic and especially monarchic-theocratic reigns, as was the Sasanian one, the royal power should be bestowed to a man in his role of supreme king-priest). The first coins with the representation of a female portrait are perhaps those struck at Ephesus from 288 to 280 B.C., that was renamed Arsinoe by Lysimachus in 295 B.C., in honour of his wife. The title of *basilissa* was conferred on the first Lysimachus's wife, Amastris, on coins of the homonymous city, but here the portrait is represented with her entire figure. Then comes the coins of Cyrene

band's, wears a high bonnet decorated on the top with a griffin's head, with two long plaits coming out from it. The smaller bust on the right, instead, wears a hat with an eagle's head (the eagle or the royal falcon is one of the natural forms of the *xwarrah*, granted by the gods to the elected kings; see *Zamyād Yašt*, or *Yašt* 19), and probably represents Anāhitā while handing to the royal couple the ribboned diadem, which is the symbol of the divine investiture. On the reverse of the coin is Wahrām, on the left of the altar, rising his right hand with the bent forefinger as a gesture of deference[42] towards Anāhitā, standing in front of him, who wears a high bonnet with an eagle's head, as also represented on the obverse of the coin, while she is holding a circular diadem to the king, symbolizing victory. Unfortunately, this last particular is corroded on our specimen.[43]

The iconographic interpretation of this issue of Wahrām II, with so many variants, put the numismatists into diffi-

---

issued by Berenikes I, or by Berenikes II, with the inscription ΒΕΡΕΝΙΚΣ ΒΑΣΙΛΙΣΣΑ (Gorini 2002). After these first instances there are many other examples, especially in Ptolemaic Egypt, and it reaches its apogee with the regal titling of Cleopatra VII, who wanted to be called ΘΕΑ ΝΕΩΤΕΡΑ on tetradrachms struck in Syria on which she was represented together with Marcus Antonius (Burnett, Amandry, & Ripollès 1992, ns. 4094-4096), or on coins with the Latin legend CLEOPATRAE REGINAE REGVM FILIORVM REGVM, "To Cleopatra, Queen of Kings (mother) of the King's sons" (Crawford 1974, n. 543/1). In comparison, on Parthian coinage appeared only the portrait of the Queen *Thea Ourania* Musa (Sellwood 1983, pl. 6, ns. 4-5), who, in 2 A.D., married her son Phraates V (or Phraataces), after having poisoned her old husband Phraates IV. He had married Musa because she had been donated to him as a slave by Augustus himself. The cunning and beautiful slave succeeded in maintaining the power for only a short period of time, due to the general indignation provoked by her cruel action that led mother and son to a ruinous end; see Bigwood 2004.

[42] Frye 1972.

[43] See Göbl 1971, pl. 4, n. 68.

culties. The study carried out by J.K. Choksy,[44] based on different kinds of sources, has offered a quite convincing exegesis about the coinage of this sovereign, even if personally I believe that there are still some doubts regarding the identification of the small figure who holds the ring, or not, on the obverse sides of the coins. In fact, it is not clear when we can refer for certain to Anāhitā or to Vərəθrayna. Not to be considered is the hypothesis of Göbl, who interpreted the series of busts on the right of the royal group as the representation of four different princes, each of them wearing personal hats. Göbl put a strong emphasis on the dynastic idea of the succession of the power and on the centrality of the royal family, imitated, as he said, from the dynastic familiar model introduced in the Roman world by the *Severi*.[45] In confirmation of his thesis, Göbl mentioned the relief of Naqš-i Rustam, in which Wahrām is represented together with three princes.

It is curious that the ring with ribbons, symbol of the royal power, is handed by a prince to the king (usually it happens to the contrary), and moreover, the ribbons are present on the rings only when divine investitures are concerned.[46] In the event that there is no presence of ribbons on the ring, it means the victory of the sovereign, as confirmed by many examples of Iranian art.[47] Indeed, the prince (Wahrām III) is represented on the coins of Wahrām, but he simply wears the Median cap and does not hand any ring to the king.[48] Instead, when the half bust

---

[44] Choksy 1989, pp. 117-135.

[45] Göbl 1971, pp. 43-45.

[46] The ribboned rings were introduced into Iranian art by the Parthians and are conferred to the king also on numerous coin types, not antecedent to the first century B.C., or by *Nike* or by a *Tyche*, but probably under the influence of the Hellenistic art.

[47] Choksy 1989, pp. 127-129.

[48] Göbl 1971, pl. 4, n. 54.

figure offers the ring, it is always represented wearing zoomorphic hats, comparable with those worn by the standing female divinity figure on the reverse.

So, in conclusion, on the obverse of the coins of Wahrām we can find:

1) Wahrām II alone.
2) Wahrām II with his wife Šābuhrduxtag.
3) Wahrām II with the prince Wahrām III.
4) Wahrām II with his wife Šābuhrduxtag and Anāhitā (Cat. n. 8), or perhaps Vərəθraɣna.

On the reverse:

1) Wahrām II with a priest or an attendant, both of them with lances.
2) Wahrām II and a "duplicate of him" (since he wears the same winged crown) at the side of the altar, both of them with lances.
3) Wahrām II paying homage to Anāhitā, raising his hand with the bent forefinger; Anāhitā hands him the ring without ribbons as symbol of victory, while on the obverse she hands him a ribboned ring (Cat. n. 8).

Therefore even if on Wahrām's coins, as Göbl underlined, it shows the principle of the royal dynasty, for the unusual, and never repeated, representation of the king beside his wife,[49] and only seldom with the prince,[50] also

---

[49] Whereas other Sasanian queens will anyhow have the privilege to issue coins: it is the queen Bōrān (629-631 A.D.), the oldest daughter of Xusraw II, and his younger sister, Āzarmīgduxt (631 A.D.). Regarding Bōrān there are fifteen different mints known and, very unusual for this period of decline, some bronze coins (mint WYHC), and even a gold *dēnār* with the representation of her frontal bust (Alram 1986, n. 927; Daryaee 1999b). On her coins it has been possible to determine three

regnal years. Unlike Āzarmīgduxt, of whom only some drachms are known (Alram 1986, n. 928), Bōrān presents also a personal crown (shaped as a calotte and decorated with three rosettes and pearls, with a diadem, and two wings on top; between them there is a globe and a crescent) and a feminine portrait with four plaits, two of them come down to the breast and the other two along her back. In comparison Āzarmīgduxt has a masculine resemblance (she's got a beard and moustache!) and looks similar, even in the crown, to the portraits of Xusraw II. This peculiar circumstance has been justified by Mochiri 1977, p. 204, who was the first one to identify a coin of Āzarmīgduxt, advancing, on one hand, with a generic statement, that in the Iranian art the female figures are rarely represented and that women wore the veil (but when they did want to represent them, they did it) and on the other hand, the scholar has proposed the hypothesis that the die had been prepared for a masculine visage so that the pretender to the throne, Farrox-Ohrmazd, could have his name engraved on the coins. The objection I raise is that the name involved is the queen's and not that of the pretender, on whose coins is the name of Ohrmazd (V or VI). If on the coin die there is the inscription Āzarmīgduxt (*'clmykdwht*), it can be supposed that they were not struck by partisans of Ohrmazd V or *sur l'ordre* of Ohrmazd. Perhaps, without relying on this improbable machination of the ambitious *spāhbed* (general), we can suppose that the minters, with only six months at their disposal, and also due to the total political confusion, were not in a position to prepare a specific die for this ephemeron queen and, therefore, they utilized an old die (probably of Xusraw II) on which they re-engraved only the name. The usage of re-engraving old dies, although not common in the first centuries of the Sasanian Empire, is documented particularly during the later empire (Tyler-Smith 2000, concerning the coins of Yazdgird III, pp. 144-145). It has to be stressed that in the Sasanian dynasty the passage of the power to female personages is not due to a kind of social emancipation during the late empire, but it is rather a matter of a precise political choice within the Iranian aristocracy which was not inclined to accept as king anybody who was not part of the royal family (Panaino 2004b: 824; Panaino 2006). Consequently, when male descendants were not available, women were chosen, and Bōrān, in particular, did her best to consolidate her authority, carrying into effect a series of political, economic, and fiscal initiatives that made her one of the most interesting figures before the final collapse of the Sasanian Empire. Regarding Bōrān's coinage see Malek & Curtis 1998, pp. 113-119, pls. 33-37.

propagandised on the reliefs, it is rather the idea of the divine transmission of royalty that is strongly put in evidence on coinage.

Moreover, we can also mention the second crown of Narseh (293-303 A.D.), that with its three twigs recalls again Anāhitā,[51] as it is confirmed by another relief of Naqš-i Rustam that represents the standing investiture of Narseh by the goddess.

In the long run, no more new elements were available and so the crowns became more and more similar to each other. Yazdgird I (399-420 A.D.) and Wahrām V (420-438 A.D.) placed a lunar crescent on the crown (connected with the astral characters of Sasanian kingship), to which Pērōz (457-484 A.D.), after his freedom from captivity from the Hephthalite Huns, added on the coins two wings at the sides, introducing his third crown.[52] Certainly, the temporary loss of the *xwarrah* and the consequent enthronement induced Pērōz to make this meaningful change of crown. His son Kawād I (first reign 488-496; second reign 499-531

---

[50] The only other case in the Sasanian coinage is the one of Ardašīr I with the young prince (Šābuhr?). See Göbl 1971, pl. 2, ns. 19-20; Alram & Gyselen 2003, Type VIII, pp. 29-31; 55-56, 132. The complete legend of this particular emission, the so-called "throne-successor coins", is very difficult to decipher.

[51] Peck 1993, p. 414; Alram 1986, n. 753; Göbl 1971, p. 45, pl. 5, ns. 75-76. The relief is illustrated in Ghirshman 1962, p. 176.

[52] See the coins in the Catalogue ns. 33-36, on which is represented the definitive type of Pērōz's crown, such as a crown with merlons, with two wings on top, with crescents and *korymbos*. The ribbons of the crown are turned upward according to an iconographic model that will also be used by his descendants, Kawād I and Xusraw I. Prior to this crown, Pērōz had two different ones: the first crown, during the two initial regnal years, with only one central merlon (at least for what it can be seen) and two crescents on the crown's cap, and the second one, from the third to the eighth regnal year, with the addition of another lateral merlon (Göbl 1971, pp. 49-50; Curtis 1999, pp. 304-306; Schindel 2004, 3/1, pp. 390-392).

A.D.), and then Xusraw I (531-579 A.D.), adopted a crown similar to the one of Pērōz, but without wings. Xusraw II (590/591-628 A.D.), starting from his second regnal year, added two wings again on the crown and also replaced the *korymbos* with a central star.

The reason for this change was certainly a political one as Xusraw in 591 succeeded in getting rid of his rebel general Wahrām Čōbīn (Wahrām VI), with the support of the Byzantines. After that Xusraw assumed the title of *pērōz*, "victorious", and added on the coins the well auspicious legend *Xusraw xwarrah abzūd*, "Xusraw (has) increased the royal glory",[53] because he henceforth was the only legitimate holder of royalty over the Iranian country (*Ērānšahr*). Consequently the adding on the crown of the wings of Vərəθraɣna and the mention of the *xwarrah*[54] resulted in a very strong message of political propaganda.[55]

The crown of Xusraw II was the iconographic model both for Yazdgird III (632-651 A.D.) and for the Arab-Sasanian coinage.[56] Indeed, it can be said that the coins of

---

[53] See the coins of the Catalogue, ns. 52-66.

[54] In the *Avesta*, the holy text of the Zoroastrian religion, the god Wahrām himself is the bearer of the *xwarrah* (*Yašt* XIV, 2). See also *Widēwdād* XIX, 37.

[55] Daryaee 1997.

[56] Not on all the first Arab-Sasanian coins are there inscriptions, in Pahlavi or in Arabic, outside the dotted rim, such as *jā'iz* (common, legal, accepted) or *bismi'llāh* (in the name of Allāh), but they can also be rather similar to the types of Xusraw II and of Yazdgird III. For example, as it was underlined by Nikitin – Roth 1995a, pp. 131-138, the year 20 of Yazdgird (651 A.D.), is as if it were "frozen", in the sense that the Arabs continued, for some years, using the dies of the last regnal year of Yazdgird. In fact, on some coins there are mints that are not compatible with the indicated regnal year as, for example, a coin of Yazdgird III of the year 20 of the mint DA (Dārābgird) that instead was invaded by the Arabs in 644 A.D. (Nikitin – Roth 1995a, p. 132, pl. 25, n. 1). Sometimes there are insignificant and not so evident iconographic particulars that reveal an Arabian manufacture, such as the inverted position of the

Yazdgird III became similar to the types of Xusraw II
(contrary to the general trend of differentiation encountered up to this time), perhaps with the aim to make them
more acceptable internally, to cope with the spreading of
the Arabs. However, these propagandistic expedients
proved to be inefficacious in facing an overwhelming enemy. The study of the coinage of Yazdgird III has recently
put into evidence[57] that after the Arab victory of al-
Qādisiyya (occurred around 635 A.D.), the coins lost uni-
formity in the style of different mints, perhaps caused by a
lower central control, and gradually some mints began to
represent the king with the beard, add a dotted rim both
on the obverse and on the reverse, changed the details of
the ear and neck ornaments and, peculiarly, starting from
the sixth and seventh year, there is a change in Yazdgird's
name. In fact, in the first three years of reign he is represented on his coins without the beard and the name is
written, in transliteration, *yzdkrty*, then there is a change in
yzdklty, so the pahlavi letter *"r"* is replaced with the letter
"l",[58] that being graphically prominent compared to the
other letters, immediately recalls the letter *"l"* contained in
the pahlavi name of Xusraw *(hwslwb)*. At that time as to-

---

attendants' hands on the sword represented on the reverse of the coins;
in fact, it is the left hand, and not the right one, as shown on the Sasanian coins, that grasps the hilt of the sword as if the guardians were
left-hand. These incongruities can be noticed on stylistic or palaeo-
graphic ground, or it is possible to notice dates that go beyond the duration of the sovereign's reign (for instance, coins of Xusraw II of the
year 69!). So these discrepancies should prevent us from making "easy"
attributions.

[57] Tyler-Smith 2000.

[58] It seems that also Alram 1986, p. 214, did not notice this in particular,
although in the table it is present the "young" bust-type (n. 931), with
the letter "r" replacing the letter "l", that in fact is clearly represented on
the coin with the "old" bust-type, featuring Xusraw II (n. 932). However, the inter-exchange of r/l in Pahlavi is a recurrent use.

day, for an inattentive or illiterate observer, it would be sufficient that the antepenultimate letter of the name was always a letter "*l*" (easier to identify), to confuse a drachm of Yazdgird with a drachm of Xusraw, and it is even more evident if we also take into consideration all the above mentioned details, in particular the crown, the beard and the multiple dotted rings.

Nevertheless, these different crowns, that we have tried to describe here, can be taken only as general chronological guides for other documents, even if they are indispensable for the study of coinage and the Sasanian ideology of power.

In fact, if one wants to analyze a late Sasanian artistic object, it will be difficult to identify for certain the king based exclusively on the crown; so, for example, among the pieces from the National Museum of Tehrān shown in Rome in July 2001, there was a silver plate with the representation of a standing king (Fig. 8)[59] that, based on the type of crown with merlons, wings and crescent, has been dated generically to the late Sasanian period or even post-Sasanian. The king is standing frontally, leaning on his sword, under an *iwān* and on a podium supported by a couple of lions. The pillars of the *iwān* are decorated with birds that are inside disks or arches and the *iwān* is surmounted by stepped merlons and there is a lunar crescent in the centre. Behind the king a large throne can be seen, with overlapped pillows. Outside the vault there are two dignitaries facing the king, with folded arms as gesture of deference. The regal crown has two merlons and it is equipped with two wings placed on top of the spherical calotte; between them there is a crescent. The wings are turned upwards, and so are the two ribbons of the big diadem fluttering behind the shoulders of the king. The

---

[59] Genito 2001, p.139.

crown type suggests a Sasanian king of late period, very likely Xusraw II, also based on the comparison with a rare gold *dēnār*, on the obverse of which is represented the frontal bust of Xusraw wearing a crown similar to the one appearing on the plate; on the reverse the king is standing and leaning on his own sword.[60]

The iconographic conception of representing the sovereign under a richly decorated *iwān* is fully supported and exalted by the famous *iwān* engraved in the rock at Tāq-i Būstān, that has been attributed to Xusraw II, as well.[61] At any rate these comparisons, even if useful, do not allow us to be sure that the plate involved is really attributable to the period of Xusraw II, as also the crowns of some following kings, as already underlined, still have the two wings and the star in the crescent on the top of the crown (like Ohrmazd V, Xusraw V and Yazdgird III). This late Sasanian iconographic mannerism went on for the first centuries of Arab domination.

In other cases, a detail of the crown can be decisive for the determination of a date. In the above mentioned exposition of the National Museum of Oriental Art in Rome, another exhibit was a plaster bust of a Sasanian king (Fig. 9)[62] coming from a Sasanian villa settled in nearby Hājiā-bād, in the Fārs. This bust has been attributed to Šābuhr II (309-379 A.D.) because of the presence of the curls that can be seen between the diadem and the crown with merlons. On the top of the crown with merlons, partly damaged, there is a flat base on which the globe of the crown was placed. On the diadem there is a decoration of two concentric circles that can be also seen, even if bigger, in the center of the straps that are crossing over the sternum. The

---

[60] Göbl 1971, pl. 14, ns. 220-221; Alram 1986, ns. 921-922.

[61] Ghirshman 1962, pp. 192-199.

[62] Genito 2001, p. 136.

ears, flanked with voluminous tufts of hair, were adorned with earrings made with two overlapping rings holding a big oval pendant, most likely a pearl. The beard, formed by little curls, is retained at the end by a ring, that lets loose a thick cluster.

On the coins Šābuhr II wears the same crown of Šābuhr I (in fact, kings with the same name used to wear the same type of crown), but he distinguishes himself just by the curls (Cat. n. 11) that characterize also the plaster bust.

In conclusion, if we cannot be as optimistic as Göbl[63] was about the fact that the Sasanian kings used to wear "personal" crowns (either because they had more than one, as the coins and literary evidence proved,[64] or because some

---

[63] Göbl 1971, p. 7, reports as follows: "Each Sasanian king had his own crown which was designed especially for him! It is to speak the guiding fossil of the entire Sasanian art and its descendants. The crown has become an infallible means of identifying the royal individual." In spite of this statement, Göbl was aware of the plurality of the crowns of some sovereigns. For example, as put in evidence with the case of Yazdgird III's coins, not always the analysis of the crown allows an immediate identification of the king. Therefore, I agree with what was stated by Peck 1993, pp. 413-415, and Daryaee 1998, p. 457: "She [Peck] rightly critiques the method of identifying rulers based on their crowns, since they had more than one crown and sometimes copied earlier monarchs."

[64] Ammianus Marcellinus, for example, writes that Šābuhr II (309-379 A.D.), during the siege of Amida in 359 A.D., "in front of his diadem worn a golden image shaped like a ram's head, with precious stones mounted on it" (XIX 1, 3: *aureum capitis arietini figmentum interstin-ctum lapillis pro diademate gestans*). A spectacular drachm of Šābuhr II wearing a helmet having ram's horns, recently published by Gyselen 2004, pp. 58-59, n. 212, demonstrates that Ammianus' tale was not fanciful, and once again that different sources must always be put together. Tabarī (Bosworth 1999, pp. 237-238) reports that Xusraw II's gold crown, due to the many additions, had become so heavy (more than 90 kilos!) that no human head could support it and therefore during the king's audiences, held in the large Hall of the Golden Throne at Ctesiphon, it was hooked to a chain coming down from the ceiling. The ring that kept the

differences are the result of free interpretation of the artist), it can, however, be claimed that numismatics is the only primary source that allows us to go through the complete evolution of Sasanian art.

1.3 The coins' iconography.

The iconography of the Sasanian coins presents a remarkable similarity if compared for instance, to Greek or Roman coins.[65] In fact, if we do not take into consideration the few emissions clearly celebrative,[66] on which the monarch is always represented, the Sasanian coins in all denominations usually show on the obverse the king's bust turned to the right and the legend written along the rim. This is contrary to the Parthian coins on which the bust is commonly turned to the left and the inscriptions are on the reverse in vertical lines around the central figure (the seated archer), forming almost a square. So the pattern of putting the inscriptions along the rim of the coin could be of Roman origin, considering that Hellenistic tradition privileges the legends in lines placed in vertical or horizontal position.

Only seldom is the bust of the sovereign represented frontally, according to an iconographic pattern properly oriental, and rarely turned to the left, perhaps by mistake. In addition to the crown already described above, the ideal

---

chain to the ceiling was extracted only in 1812 (Christensen 1944, pp. 466-469).

[65] However, the repeating of the types, such as the king's bust on the obverse and the fire altar on the reverse, is converted in an incredible series of variants, more or less significant, that make the study of Sasanian numismatics rather complex.

[66] I have already mentioned the gold coins issued on the occasion of the investiture of the king or evocating the *xwarrah*. The frontal posture of the king was, in these cases, preferred.

king is shown most of the time with a beard with the exception of Ardašīr III, 628-629 A.D., who was a child,[67] and the first emissions of Yazdgird III. He wears the pearl earrings (about the precious pearl worn by Pērōz, there is a fine tale in Proc. *BP* I 4, 14-31), a necklace, a ring into which the end of his beard is retained and a close-fitting dress that gives evidence of the large breast and shoulders. The garment is always crossed near the sternum point by two broad decorated bands centrally tied by a jewel of circular shape. On the well preserved specimens, some linear decorations and symbols can be seen, meaning that the tunic was richly embroidered as it is shown, for example, on many silver plates. Usually the bands on the cloth are decorated with dots. From Xusraw I (531-579 A.D.) on, in the coin field there is a crescent-star combination.

Up to the end of the third century A.D., the Sasanian coins include rather physiognomic portraits, considering that Roman portraits during the late empire also tend to idealize and to fix the visages not within naturalistic schemes (for example, the tetrarchs are quite difficult to distinguish from one another), and then proceed with some representations that purely symbolize the ideal image of the sovereign, as does Byzantine coinage.[68]

---

[67] Ardašīr III was only a seven year old boy when he ascended the throne. However Šābuhr II, although he was elected king while still an embryo in his mother (Agathias IV 25), was always represented with a beard, perhaps because that was the look expected for the ideal Sasanian king.

[68] In the Byzantine coinage the individual features are very rare and they are just evident with the representation of different beards and haircuts (Grierson 1982, pp. 29-30). The first Byzantine emperor to be represented with the beard is Phocas (602-610 A.D.). This could have been done either to add a realistic element to the portrait, in order to affect his subjects, or to differentiate him from the previous emperors since he was an usurper of barbarian descent, coming from the lower

During the third century the volumes of the figures are more marked and evident, either on the obverse or on the reverse of the coins, then they tend to go toward a plain (and sometimes confused) decorative linearism that, in a certain way, preludes Islamic art.

One of the peculiarities of the Sasanian coins is the multiple dotted rims. The issues begin with only one rim on the obverse, while double and triple dotted rims appear on bronze coins of Šābuhr II (309-379 A.D.). Then Walaxš (484-488 A.D.) introduces a double rim on the obverse of the silver drachms and this will become a characteristic on all the coins starting from Xusraw II. Outside the dotted rim, Kawād I, from his second reign (499-531 A.D.), puts the motif of the crescent and the star (present also over his shoulders), that is positioned and corresponds to three of the cardinal points (at 3, 6, 9 o'clock), while the first cardinal point could be represented by the crescent just placed on the king's crown. Also the following kings maintain this astral iconography. Only Xusraw I (531-579 A.D.) and Wahrām VI (590-591 A.D.) again put the crescents without stars, out of the dotted rim.

Although it is very difficult to explain the meaning of such recurrent astral symbolism, it is likely that it should be connected with the Zoroastrian religion and with the cosmic kingship.[69] The multiple dotted rims could in fact represent the three celestial spheres (corresponding to the good thoughts, good words and good deeds) of the Zoroastrian uranography, if we consider them in relation to the stars and crescents; but they could also transmit the idea of

---

ranks of the army. But also the "Persian" fashion could have influenced the Byzantine tyrant.

[69] Göbl 1983a, p. 328.

the *xwarrah* as a luminous halo.[70] I think a very interesting hypothesis is one that considers crescents and stars (usually represented with six points) as simply alluding to the sun and the moon.[71] Such an interpretation fits the conception of the Sasanian royalty very well, according to which the king is the one whose *čihr* comes from the gods in the official regal titling *kē čihr az yazdān*, usually translated in "whose origin/seed is from the gods", ἐκ γένους θεων, according to the Greek version. However, the pahlavi term *čihr*, besides meaning of seed and origin, means also "visible form",[72] and only the intrinsic meaning of such a word can explain, for example, the regal titling that Šābuhr II uses as a presentation in an epistle (357 A.D.) to the Roman emperor Constantius: *Rex regum Sapor, particeps siderum, frater Solis et Lunae* (Amm. Marc. XVII 5, 3); "I Sapor, King of Kings, partner of the stars, brother of the sun and of the moon". The sun and the moon, together with the stars, are the only visible divine entities in the Zoroastrian theology, and their nature is beneficent and positive, whereas in opposition the nature of the planets is demoniac, according to Sasanian astrology.[73] The king has the same *čihr*, the same

---

[70] This last hypothesis has been suggested, for example, by Daryaee 1997, pp. 46-47.

[71] It is an interpretation briefly advanced by Malek & Curtis 1998, page 117, note 24. See Gariboldi 2004a and Panaino 2004a, pp. 578-579.

[72] MacKenzie 1971, p. 22, sub *čihr* and *čihr(ag)*; Panaino 2003a.

[73] Although the planets (in the ancient astrology the Sun and Moon are also included under this category) had a divine nature in Greek and Mesopotamic conception, in the Zoroastrian tradition they were considered of evil nature. The reasons were mainly two: the first one, according to astrology, is that the planets have an uncertain nature, either positive or negative, and this vagueness was not acceptable for the religion; the second one, is due to the motion itself of the planets, sometimes retrograde, and as a consequence identifiable with the cosmic disorder provoked by Ahreman, in opposition to the order represented by the fixed stars. Nevertheless, in the Pahlavi texts, Jupiter-Ohrmazd

divine visible form of the sun and of the moon, as results from the analysis of Greek-Byzantine and Armenian literary sources.[74] In the Armenian sources, for instance, in Movsēs Xorenac'i III 17 (around the fifth century A.D.), there is the concept that the king is "equal to the sun" (*barjakic' aregakan*, literally "the one who sits on the same seat of the sun"), and there is also the mention of oaths to the sun (*arew*).[75] Moreover, in a letter sent in 590 A.D. from Xusraw II to the general Wahrām Čōbīn, there is the following statement concerning the king: "among the gods a righteous and eternal man, among men a god most remarkable... rising together with the sun and bestowing eyes on the night" (Theoph. Simoc. IV 8).

A further confirmation of the connection between the divine "visible form" of the sovereign and the sun and the moon, also comes from the supposed correspondence between human microcosm and macrocosm that are listed,

---

and Venus-Anāhīd are considered of beneficent influence and, in accordance with the Greek tradition, the sun (M.P. *Xwarxšēd*) and the moon (M.P. *Māh*) exerted positive influence against the malefic planets (*Dēnkard* III, 192 and 263). See Raffaelli 2001, pp. 19-20; Panaino 1999.

[74] Panaino 2004a.

[75] Moses of Khoren II 19; III 26; III 42; see Huyse 2006, p. 193. Also Malalas (449, 44) reports a letter of Kawād I to Justinian I, written in 529 A.D.: "Kawād, King of those who are ruling, of the rising sun, to Flavius Justinian Caesar, of the setting moon". With this metaphor the two empires are assimilated to the sun and the moon. Very interesting also is a passage of Petrus Chrysologus, bishop of Ravenna in the fifth century A.D., who confirms these astral patterns of the Sasanian kingship (*Sermo* 120, 2; *Patrol. Lat.* 527): *persarum reges* [...] *nunc radiato capite, ne sint homines, solis resident in figura; nunc inpositis sibi cornibus, quasi viros se doleant, effeminantur in lunam; nunc varias velut siderum sumunt formas, ut hominis perdant figuras.* "The Persian Kings... now with a radiant head, they sit in the image of the sun, as though they were not humans; now, putting horns on themselves, as if they were regretting to be men, they become like women in the moon; now they assume various forms like those of the stars in order to lose their human shape."

for example in the *Bundahišn* (28, 4), the Middle-Persian book of the "primordial creation", in which the two asters are just collocated imaginarily as if they were in the same position of the man's eyes.[76] It has to be added that the astrology attributed to the stars is also a domain over the cardinal directions,[77] and this could also explain the reason for which the symbols of the sun and the moon on the Sasanian coins are placed in correspondence to them.

In conclusion, I would like to draw attention to some coins, not widely known, of two kings of Persis, such as Nambed and Napād:[78] these coins clearly represent the image of the king with an entire or half bust figure in front of a six pointed star (the sun, with six points as represented on the Sasanian coins) and a lunar crescent. Clearly, the pre-Sasanian Persis kingship was already deeply connected and expressed through the sun and the moon and the Sasanians, as I have already underlined, continued this

---

[76] Such correspondence of the eyes to the sun and the moon has been stated also in the "hermetic" Greek texts (*Iatromathematikà* 1, 5). See Raffaelli 2001, pp. 45-46, note 38.

[77] In the *Bundahišn* V 3-4 and II 3-4, four fixed stars, positioned like a "general" (M.P. *spāhbed*) of each cardinal point, fight separately against a planet when Ahreman launches the attack (Panaino 1999; Raffaelli 2001, pp. 99-101). According to this belief, the sun and the moon, contrary to the astrological tradition, are not considered planets but fixed stars and maintain their positive influence as they are Ohrmazd's creations. In order to reach the number of seven planets, the sun and the moon are replaced with the black sun and the black moon. The importance of the cardinal directions in the Sasanian cultural tradition is also evident in some Pahlavi texts which describe the presence of four generals, each of them in charge of the supervision of one region (M.P. *kust*) of the empire (Daryaee 2003), a military and administrative reform wanted by Xusraw I. The real existence of four commanders has been definitively documented by the personal seals of the *spāhbed*s (Gyselen 2001). Gnoli 1985 had already advanced the historical foundation of this military quadripartition, based on the analysis of some Pahlavi texts.

[78] Alram 1986, ns. 599-611.

same tradition. Indeed, the sun and the moon on these coins seems to take the place of the ever-burning fire, iconography often represented on the coinage of Persis that was adopted *in toto* by the Sasanians.

If we add to these iconographic motives the use of writing the legends in Aramaic, differing from the Parthians who have a predilection for Greek, I think it is unquestionable that the Sasanian coinage comes from one of the Fratarakas kings of Persis. In this view, the Sasanians broke with the Parthians, claiming their independence from them and the Greek tradition, but they kept on with the culture, language and religious beliefs of the Persian dynasts, succeeding in conferring on them a strongly nationalistic dimension.

At the beginning, the reverse of the Sasanian coins have only one dotted rim. Šābuhr II introduces a double and triple rim on his copper coins, but they will be used instead on silver coinage starting from Xusraw II. So his coins have double dotting on the obverse, and a triple rim on the reverse. Xusraw II introduces the motif of the crescent and the star placed outside the margins, and also on the reverse. Kawād has two circles on the reverse only during his last decade of reign.

All these particularities, in addition to testifying to a complex system of symbols concerning royal power and religion, are useful for dating the coins. As previously said, in an initial phase the figures on the coins are better defined and only with a few additions but, in the long run, we have the introduction of star-crescent motifs, and they are placed, alternatively, inside or outside the coin field or sometimes there are crescents without stars, simple or double or even triple rims on the obverse or on the reverse. I suggest that all of this was probably done with the purpose to help the users to distinguish the coins of each king, and moreover we cannot forget that the legends were only understood by a small number of people, and often they were abbreviated and sometimes even wrong. This portrayal of varying and particulars of the royal crown was aimed to satisfy the desire of the Sasanian kings of an easier identification.

Usually, on the reverse of the coins there is representation of the Zoroastrian fire altar. There are three principle variants: the fire altar alone, the altar with two attendants and the altar with two attendants and, over it, a bust upon the flames. Ardašīr I introduced the first type that is formed by an altar column, sometimes engraved with three parallel lines, placed on a stepped base. The top of the altar is supported by four paw lion holders with ribbons but only two of them are visible on the coins due to the frontal perspective. But already Šābuhr I introduced two lateral attendants, the meaning of which is not yet completely clear. In particular, for their symmetric disposition it is wondered if they were added only for decorative needs. Initially these figures are represented with lances or they hold the Zoroastrian sacred bundle, the *barsom*. Their heads are facing either the altar or the opposite part. From Xusraw I onward they stand frontally, at first leaning on their lances and then on short sticks or swords. With Wahrām II (276-293 A.D.) at least one of the two figures seems to represent the king, based on the crown he wears and a double representation of the king can also be seen. The presence of the bust upon the flames is represented only between the reigns of Ohrmazd II (303-309 A.D.) and Walaxš (484-488 A.D.), but discontinuously.[79] Even the interpretation of this bust is problematic. In some cases it seems to refer to the king who could have founded

---

[79] On the coins of the Catalogue, the bust in the flames is represented on the ns. 9-26 (Šābuhr II, Šābuhr III, Wahrām IV), and 37-38 (Walaxš).

new sacred fires.[80] But if the bust is not crowned, it has been agreed that perhaps it is the representation of Ohrmazd or of the *xwarrah*, the regal halo.

An alternative hypothesis has been advanced by Gnoli,[81] who has identified the bust with Zoroaster himself based on a passage of Dio Chrisostom (*Oratio* XXXVI 40) which tells that Zoroaster got out from a fire storm without any damage and that he revealed the true religion not to everybody, but only to those who were obviously disposed to the truth and to the comprehension of God, those who the Persians used to call Magi.[82] Evidently fire does not burn the just men. The fires were collocated on high places, as also Herodotus relates (I 131).

So, in representing on the coins the teaching the prophet placed upon the flames, the Sasanian kings would have professed their Zoroastrian faith. The identification of the bust upon the flames is, at any rate, still problematic. After king Narseh (293-303 A.D.) on the altar column are two fluttering ribbons, turning downward or upward.

A very important feature that appears on the reverse of the Sasanian coins is the indication of the mint, usually starting from Wahrām IV (388-399 A.D.), even if the mint-mark appears regularly only with Wahrām V (420-438

---

[80] From the trilingual inscription of Šābuhr I we have learned that, for instance, the king established five sacred fires: one was given his name and the other four the names of his sons. One thousand lambs were donated to each fire annually and some bread and wine were offered in sacrifice each day in favour of the soul of the sovereign (M.P. *pad amā ruwān*) and the members of the royal family, alive or dead, of which there was a list with corresponding honorific titles. The importance of the fire foundations (Macuch 2004) in the political, economic, and religious life of the Sasanian society was great and, in a certain sense, justifies the presence of the fire altar on the coins for the whole duration of the dynasty.

[81] Gnoli 1966.

[82] Panaino 2004b.

A.D.), and it is placed in the coin field at the right. Before Wahrām V, the sign of the mint can be seen above the fire altar, on the left, or engraved on the shaft of the altar. The exact number and the identifications of the mints is one of the principal problems of Sasanian numismatics that is still open and a topic to which we will return.

The reverses are very important because they allow us to date the coins exactly. In fact, starting from Zāmāsp (496-499 A.D.) and from the eleventh year of Kawād I (499/500 A.D.), the engraving of the regnal year of the sovereign was introduced. Therefore, from the second reign of Kawād, on the Sasanian coins we can always see the date on the left, between the attendant and the rim, written in Middle-Persian.

Finally, a very important standardization of the coins had been reached with the indication on the reverse of the issuing mint, at the right, and of the regnal year, at the left.

Among the most unusual emissions concerning the coinage involved some copper coins of Kawād I which stand out for their singularity, but with the dimension of a drachm, with a double portrait. Up to a few years ago, only one specimen was known to have been published and interpreted by Göbl[83] as a drachm of Kawād I celebrating a victory on the Iranian Huns and at whose court a member of the Sasanian royal family was eventually designed as local king. The hypothesis of the Austrian scholar was based on the fact that the figure on the reverse was represented with its raised hand, just like a similar posture the Huns used to represent on their coins. It has to be noted that on the specimen analysed by Göbl the legends were poorly visible and no mint or date signs had been en-

---

[83] Göbl 1971, p. 20, Pl. 11, n. 192; Alram 1986, n. 902.

graved. The Mochiri's publication,[84] concerning ten more similar coins, allows us to carry out some considerations. First of all, these coins are not silver but copper and it is even doubtful that they can be defined as real coins, since they lack the mint-mark and the regnal year.

On the obverse, the bust of Kawād I is always represented according to his traditional iconography. On the reverse there is a half bust of a male figure who is represented on some coins wearing a Phrygian cap and on other coins with curly hair shaped like a Phrygian cap. His right arm is raised, covered with a sleeve, and the hand, just a little bit at a higher level compared to the shoulder, has three straight fingers and the thumb touches the forefinger, in accordance with a classic attitude represented also on the Sasanian seals, picturing the act of pronouncing a votive formula. On two specimens the head of the male figure is surrounded by a nimbus, so Mochiri has advanced the hypothesis that it could be Mithra.

The compared analysis of the coins, all of them badly preserved due also to the fragility of the metal, allows us to interpret the inscription referring to the God's words as: *šahrewar yazd, translated by Mochiri as "God (grants) the ideal empire".[85] Šahrewar (Av. Xšaθra Vairya) is also the name of one of the six Aməša Spənta (in Middle-Persian *Amahraspand*), who joints Ohrmazd in the fight against Ahreman, with the role of keeper of the metals and arms.[86]

---

[84] Mochiri 1998b, pp. 45-54, Pls. 3-7. About these puzzling copper emissions of Kawād, see now Schindel 2004, 3/1, pp. 465-466; Gyselen 2004, pp. 62-63, n. 265.

[85] Mochiri 1998b, p. 52. *Šahrewar* has been translated literally by MacKenzie 1971, p. 79, with "the best rule".

[86] Cereti 2001, pp. 59, 94, 102; Gray 1929, pp. 45-47. *Šahrewar* is very difficult to interpret unless it is considered a proper name; in the Pahlavi texts it always designates the name of the god and in some cases it is

Therefore, we have to add to the hypothesis of Mochiri (it is Mithra that pronounces the motto), also the possibility that *Šahrewar yazd* could be instead a kind of explanation concerning the figure of just the god *Šahrewar*. Since he is the metal keeper, perhaps his presence on the coins could not be considered so obsolete. The fact that *Šahrewar*'s head is represented on some coins surrounded by a nimbus, can probably be connected with a passage of the *Avesta* which says "he looks like the sun" (*Yasna* 43.16). Curiously, on the coins there is an additional inscription on the reverse outside the dotted rim and it is the first time that it appears on the Sasanian coins (while the inscriptions on the external rim will be characteristic of the Arab-Sasanian coinage). The obverse is usually without any inscription but in some cases, on the outer rim, *abzōn*, "increase" is legible; but I think that there should be written also the name of Kawād.

However, the most interesting inscription is the one placed on the reverse outside the dotted rim, that could be interpreted as *Kawād *frāxwēnīdār*, "Kawād giver of a prosperous life", possibly to be put in relation with the "desirable reign" (*Šahrewar*) to which alludes the internal inscription. Therefore, the whole message of these propagandistic inscriptions seems to insist on a desirable condition of serenity during a period that was full of rather tough religious and social troubles. Could this emission, as Mochiri has suggested, come from a context not connected with the Zoroastrian orthodoxy and elaborated in the period during which Kawād joined the Communist theories of Mazdak, while drought and famine were occurring? At the present time this hypothesis remains suggestive, even if it is not demonstrable, until we are able to recognize all

---

used on seals as a personal name even by private persons (Gignoux 1986, p. 163, n. 869).

the variations of these copper emissions, which Schindel has recently dated between the years 13 and 19 of the reign of Kawād. He relates them, following Göbl, to the victories, or to some political achievement of the king, against the Hephthalites in the East.

1.4 Denominations and weights.

As concerns the denominations and the weights of the coins, at least at the beginning, the Sasanians continued the tradition of ancient Greek origin (but not regarding the iconography and the language, as it has been underlined above), but also the local monetary tradition of Persis, based especially on the silver fractions of the drachm. So the basic silver coin, the drachm, reached under Ardašīr the theoretic medium weight of the Attic drachm of 4.12 g (actually, the Sasanian drachms fluctuate from about 3 to 4.25 g),[87] and the intrinsic quality of the metal is very good. Also, the Parthians adopted the Attic drachm, especially for trade reasons, which was imported in great quantities in the Orient by Alexander the Great,[88] and had influenced heavily the economic relations in the whole Mediterranean basin and the Near East.

---

[87] The metrological studies for the Sasanian coinage, especially for the low denominations, are still rather insufficient. Instead for what concerns the silver drachm, that was the fundamental monetary unit, see Gyselen 1989c, pp. 5-23, who has analyzed the treasure of Susa which is important not only because it consists of 1171 coins, of which 1168 are of Xusraw II, but also because it was hoarded during the Sasanian period (probably in 626 AD.). Based on the treasure of Susa, the average weight of the drachms in this period varied from 4. 00g to 4. 20g with only a few specimens exceeding this weight. For details on Sasanian denominations and weights, see now Alram – Gyselen 2003, pp. 162-170; Schindel 2004, 3/1, pp. 99-120.

[88] Vickers 1995, pp. 176-178.

It has to be remembered that the most important trans-actions, during the Parthian and Sasanian period, were carried out with silver coins whereas the coins in poor metal were used for local daily needs. The Sasanians minted abundantly silver coins. Ardašīr issued also half-drachms and obols (the obol is called in Middle-Persian *dān(ag)*, "seed", "grain"), with the value of a sixth of a drachm, always in silver, but the issue of these coins was stopped (at least basing on the findings) in this order: the half-drachm after Wahrām II (276-293 A.D.), and the silver obol after Kawād I. Göbl maintained[89] that these fractions of the drachm had been issued for celebrative purposes or for being distributed to the crowd, as happened sometimes on the occasion of the *congiarii* or when the Roman em-peror granted deeds of *li-beralitas*. Certainly they were quite limited issues, but my opinion is that these minor fractions probably did not fully meet the needs of the daily trade.

During the reign of Wahrām II the issue of the silver tetradrachms (four drachms value) was also stopped. The tetradrachms (a kind of coin widely used in the Hellenistic age and also used by the Romans in the most important Oriental provinces, such as Asia, Syria and Egypt) became, in the long run, more and more debased; in fact, the last tetradrachms issued by the Parthians, as it happened for the Sasanian ones, contain a very high percentage of cop-per, so it happens that sometimes they appear of poor metal.

The fractions of the copper obol and of the silver drachm are rare, and come to an end gradually after Šābuhr II (309-379 A.D.), even if there are some copper coins of Yazdgird III,[90] so it is likely that some pieces were

[89] Göbl 1983a, p. 329 and Göbl 1971, p. 27.
[90] Tyler-Smith 2000, p. 136.

issued, anyway, during the late Sasanian period, but they
are of small module and weight, with special reverse types
too. However, we have to underline that the Sasanian copper coinage is quite neglected and any consideration must
be expressed within generic terms.

As a matter of fact, it is almost unknown either the
value subdivision of the copper coins, that were evidently
different, or the names attributed to the coins, or even their
relation with silver. The only known denomination for the
copper coins is the *pišīz*, but it is not clear what fraction of
the obol relates to, or, for instance, if it could be perhaps
compared to the Greek term χαλκους, with the generic
meaning of "small change".

From excavation coin findings we know that during the
Sasanian period in Persia there was still available a large
quantity of small bronze units, both Parthian or Hellenistic,[91] used for daily purchases, and consequently there was
no need to make a massive production of these coins. In
order to have a general view of the situation, we have to
consider the fact that some coins of very poor value could
have been struck in lead, a metal cheaper than copper. A
distinction has to be made between the cases in which the
lead is added to the alloy (and the quantity should not be
higher than 5%), or those in which the coin is totally made
of lead. For example, Sasanian lead coins have been found
during the French excavations at Masjid-i Soleiman, and
especially the coins of Šābuhr II are quite numerous, but it
has to be remembered that some lead coins in the name of

---

[91] For example, during excavations carried out at Qasr-i Abu Nasr, in
the Fārs, some bronze coins of Hellenistic period of Alexander the Great
and Seleucus I have been found as were coins of the kingdom of Persis,
together with Elymaean and Sasanian coins. See Frye 1973, pp. 26-27, Pl.
1; Miles 1959, p. 19, Pl. I, 1.

Ardašīr I are already known.[92] Some lead pieces could be ancient forgeries, but in most of the cases the coins involved are official, complementary and substitutive of the copper denominations, when in the local market there was a shortage of such coins. In the Persian Gulf area the use of lead coins was particularly abundant during the Islamic period. Also, in Byzantine coinage some lead coins can be found especially between the sixth and seventh centuries, which were issued in "emergency" areas, such as Cilicia and Syria, during the troubles which occurred under Phocas and the advancing of the Persian army in the reign of Heraclius.[93]

The Sasanian kings, following the Achaemenid tradition, also issued gold coins whereas the Parthians did not. Modern scholars usually believe that Sasanian gold coins were minted only for festive and commemorative purposes and that gold was never part of the general currency, with no relation with silver coinage, as advanced by Göbl.[94] This opinion is justified by the evidence of the small numbers of the surviving gold specimens and that sometimes gold coins have special typologies. Notwithstanding this picture, there are elements to think that besides a ceremonial character, Sasanian *dēnār*s had also economic value with a precise relation in silver, as I have pointed out on several occasions. First of all, it is not true that approximately half of the Sasanian monarchs coined the *dēnār*, as we generally read in modern literature, since at least twenty-two kings coined gold (73%). The last new *dēnār* discovered is of Wistahm (591/592-597 A.D.). The

---

[92] Morrison 1993. Regarding the Sasanian coins, see in particular the pages 89-90, 93-94, with the figure n. 10 that reproduces a lead tetradrachm of Ardašīr I found in the above mentioned excavations.

[93] Morrison 1993, pp. 91-92.

[94] Göbl 1971, pp. 27-29; for a divergent opinion, see Gariboldi 2006, pp. 55-87 and Gariboldi (forthcoming 2009).

Saeedi's collection is very important because it contains, for the first time, the same die used for the reverse by two kings in succession, such as some *dēnār*s of Wahrām I and of Wahrām II, and Šābuhr III and Wahrām IV.[95] This implies to me, at least in these cases, a sort of serial production of gold coins. Under Šābuhr II and Pērōz gold production was more abundant, and probably it was used as a means of payment in Eastern Iran, where gold coins were used in this way as is testified, for example, by the Bactrian legal documents.

Special attention should be paid to the weight of the coins, in fact, from Ardašīr I to Šābuhr II the *dēnār* had a weight similar to the Roman *aureus*, of about 7. 20g, instead Šābuhr II (309-379 A.D.) or Šābuhr III (383-388 A.D.), started to issue gold coins following, more or less, the standard of the Roman *solidus*, of about 4.25g. (the so called light-weight *dēnār*s). Is it possible that the new light-weight Sasanian gold coin had no relation with the *solidus* at the 1/72 of *libra* (4.5g), which was introduced in the Roman monetary system by the reform of Constantine? Likely, the light-weight *dēnār* introduced after Šābuhr II had little to do, in itself as a gold piece, with questions of propaganda, but there are arguments to believe, as Schindel[96] has freshly noted, that the Sasanian *dēnār*s were coined on a metrological basis in some way reckoning in carats, as the Roman *solidus*. However that may be, the last known *dēnār* fraction (1/6) belongs to Kawād, and it could be probably compared to a Roman *tremissis*. After Xusraw II the production of gold coins stopped, even if it is known a celebrative *dēnār* of queen Bōrān (630-631 A.D.). The gold and silver coins issued by Bōrān are even mentioned in the *Chronicle of Seert*. Other arguments supporting the thesis of

---

[95] Gyselen 2004, p. 68.
[96] Schindel 2004, p. 99.

an economic value of the *dēnār*, or, more in general, showing the use of gold in the Sasanian economy, can be learned in Pahlavi and Greek literature and also from a Sasanian seal of a *zarrbed*, "master of the gold", a charge probably conceived for the exploitation of mines in Armenia, "which is the place where the Persians mine gold, that they take to the king" (Proc. *BP* I 15, 18). Moreover, large amounts of gold and silver were given by the Romans to the Sasanian Empire as ransoms, tributes, and State subsidies. It is reasonable to believe that the Sasanians did not intend to be out of the international market. Mesopotamia and Iran had for centuries been the bridge for the passage of any kind of goods between East and West along the so called "Silk Road". So it seems unlikely that during the Sasanian period there was no need to possess coins of high value, in order to carry out trade of luxury articles and to pay mercenary troops and foreign merchants. It is an ascertainable fact that the Sasanians did not issue a large number of gold coins, nevertheless they made a lot of silver plates, most of them coming from outer Iran, on which there is usually an indication of the exact weight that is comparable to the standard of the Attic drachm.[97] Therefore, the silver plates could be considered as "high-denominations", of easy transportation and negotiability either for their intrinsic value or for their unquestionable artistic beauty. Along with their nature of being objects particularly adept for royal *donativa*, silver plates have a precise economic value and can be given on pledge, according with the Sasanian law book (MHD 101, 17-102, 3), instead of money. In this specific case one vase (M.P. *yām*) was conveyed as a pledge against ten *stērs*. But in the MHD we find also the proof that gold in bullion played an important role as a form of payment in private life. In a

---

[97] Vickers 1995, in particular, pp. 182-184.

chapter concerning payments from the family estate, one "must convey half in gold and half in silver" (MHD 18, 1-6: *ud nēm zarr ud nēm asēm dahišn*). Another example is the Sasanian silver bowl found in a tomb during regular excavations at Armazi, the ancient capital of Georgia.[98] The inscription engraved on the bowl refers to Pābag the *bitaxš* (a kind of viceroy who took care of the possessions of the king of Persia) son of Georgian governors of Sasanian origin, and it says also that this object is:

> '*symy s xx xx x iii* ZWZN *i*, "silver (not coined) (equals to) 53 staters and 1 drachm".

The word in Middle Persian *asēm*, "silver", comes from the Greek technical term ἄσημον, an adjective that, accompanied to a noun of a metal, means "raw, not coined". It follows the abbreviation *s* for the staters, an important weight unit equal to 4 drachms, always of Greek origin (in Greek στατήρ, in MP. *stēr*). In some cases the word "stater" can also be expressed through the Aramaic heterogram MCY.[99] After the number of the staters, in this case 53, that are indicated with the x and the vertical short lines follow the units of minor value such as the drachms, that are always indicated in Parthian and in Middle-Persian, with the ideogram ZWZN,[100] in Middle-Persian *drahm*, in Greek

---

[98] Henning 1961, pp. 353-356.

[99] Skjærvø & Harper 1993, p. 188; Skjærvø 1997, pp. 93-104.

[100] Such a heterogram can be seen not only on vases, for instance, but also on Sasanian *ostraca* on which are reported the payments and transactions of material goods. During the seventh century, on Pahlavi *ostraca* found at Shiraz belonging to the archives of a trader who entered the credits in favour of him for the sales of barley, the heterogram is abbreviated with two vertical lines (ZZ) that always stand for ZWZN. For each sale of barley, the trader was in credit of one or two drachms. Unfortunately, the quantity of barley corresponding to the money that

δραχμή. Sometimes, on Sasanian vases we can also find the word *sang*, "weight", or *saxt* "weighted" (heterogram YNGDWN), which precedes *asēm*. So the bowl of Armazi, that actually weights 850 g, was worth 213 drachms (53 x 4 + 1) by the Sasanians, with a stater of 15.96g and a drachm of 3.99g. We have to note the precise attention that was given to calculate the weight expressed in drachms. I remember that in the eschatological Pahlavi text *Ardā Wirāz Nāmag* (AWN 27; 67; 80), atrocious infernal punishments were inflicted on those who did not respect, in the worldly life (M.P. *gētīg*), the official weights (MP. *sang*).

Considering such economic *patterns*, the lack of "high-denominations", the so called *penuria auri*, seems to be less macroscopic than one could figure out based on the shortage of Sasanian gold coins. Another curiosity about the bowl of Armazi suggests a further explanation on the use of the gold coins: an *aureus* was found inside the vessel of the emperor Valerianus. As we can see, foreign coins could have also been used obviously based on their intrinsic value. The use of local coins together with foreign ones was rather widespread during late antiquity and the medieval period.[101] The *aureus* of Valerianus, by which it is possible to date the tomb at the end of the third century A.D., could have been chosen by the Sasanians in remembrance of their victories, and we should not be surprised if this piece is part of a plunder or a ransom paid by the Romans.

Moreover, it cannot be excluded that, as testified by the hoard of Humeina from Southern Jordan,[102] the Sasanians, instead issuing gold coins in large quantities, preferred

---

the buyers owed to the trader was not reported on the *ostraca*. See Harmatta 1976, pp. 225-237.

[101] Raschke 1978, pp. 734-736.

[102] De Bruijn & Dudley 1995.

sometimes to imitate the Byzantine *solidi*, which had a very high margin of acceptability, much more than the Sasanian coins. In fact, the hoard consists of 5 gold *solidi* of Arcadius (383-408 A.D.), from the mint of Constantinople, and 18 silver drachms of Yazdgird I (399-420 A.D.).[103] However, the *solidi* had been clearly imitated by some clandestine Sasanian mint (they weighed 4.25g, a Persian standard) that was not accustomed to writing in Latin and may be settled in Iran, or possibly in Hīra, the capital of the vassal kingdom of the Lakhmids, according to Schindel. If, based on new data, it could be possible to show that other Byzantine *solidi* were forgeries of Sasanian production, the problem of the shortage of the Sasanian gold coins would be partially solved. I also stress that the *solidi* involved were not imitated for profit, since they comply with the weight and the good quality of the metal of the official coins but were probably created in order to have local spending money.

1.5 Mints and circulation of the coins.

The number of the mints in the Sasanian Empire varied from time to time according to the needs and the growth of the *Ērānšahr*. At the beginning, during the reign of Ardāšir, there could have been two or three mints located in the west of Iran, such as Staxr, in the first phase, and then Hamadān (Ecbatana) and the capital Seleucia-Ctesiphon, which were already operative under the Parthians. In the fourth century A.D., after the military campaigns led by Šābuhr II in the East, the number of the mints grew even higher in the Orient as far as present-day Afghanistan. For example, in 1933 at Tepe Maranjān (Kabul) a hoard containing 326 drachms of Šābuhr II was found, most of them

---

[103] Schindel 2004, 3/1, pp. 502-506.

being of semi-local production.[104] The most productive mint was Ctesiphon/Kabul, but in Eastern Iran Sakastān, Marw and Herat were also operative in this period.

However, in a few cases during the period of Wahrām I and Šābuhr II, only from Wahrām IV (388-399 A.D.) the mint-mark is generally indicated, as it has been already mentioned, on the reverse, usually abbreviated with two or three letters (rarely four). Before this period the name of the mint, if indicated, could have been written also in full, in particular Marw (MLWY), on some coins of Šābuhr I and II, and Sakastān (SKSTN) on coins of Wahrām I[105] and Šābuhr II. Unsigned drachms were minted until the reign of Yazdgird II. The exact number of the mints, the correct reading and, in particular, their location, has not been fully verified until to now. During the period of violent wars or when the empire was at the top of its prosperity, the number of mints working contemporaneously could have even been forty, just as during the age of Xusraw II (590/591-628 A.D.). In total it is possible to count almost a hundred different mint signs, but the fact has to be considered that some signs graphically similar could indicate the same mint, and so the number of mints gets remarkably lower; then there is also the possibility that some mints, during an administrative reform, could have changed their name or, moreover, a certain mint could have been working under certain kings and inert in other periods. For example, both AY and AYL could indicate Susa, even if the identification is hypothetic, while AYLAN should be Ērān-āsān-kar-Kawād. The administrative glyptic has evidenced great changes in the provincial administration of the empire and especially, in a remarkable way, during the reigns of Kawād I and Xusraw I, who made a very important series of

---

[104] Malek 1993, p. 243; Göbl 1984; Schindel 2004, 3/1, p. 223.
[105] Nikitin 1999, p. 263, fig. 1a.

fiscal and military reforms after the cruel repression of Mazdak's revolt.[106]

Some mint-marks are localised for certain, such as ART for Ardašīr-xwarrah, BYŠ for Bīšābuhr, AHM for Hamadām, LD for Ray, but a lot of others are still waiting for an attribution. We have to notice that in the last years the efforts made by scholars have brought good results, especially from the analysis of the official seals, on which very often is the name of the city either in the centre (in an abbreviated form), or along the rim (written in full), thus the identification of some mints have been possible.[107] Unfortunately, the administrative seals do not antedate Kawād I, since probably he was the one who widely introduced such a system,[108] for which there is a considerable gap during the first centuries of the empire. Moreover, in spite of the high number of provinces during the late empire, the number of mints is lower, so it is evident that not all the provinces had their own mint with the exception of the South of Iran where there is a close parallelism between provinces and mints.[109] This situation could have been the result of a better bureaucratic organization for a geographic area of extreme importance; in fact, Fārs and Kermān are the historical and political heart of the Sasanian kingdom.

In addition to the stable mints there was also an important travelling mint, that had to follow the king during his movements, which is indicated with the heterogram

---

[106] Gyselen 1989a; Gyselen 1989b; Gyselen 1979; Rubin 1995; Sears 1999; Gyselen 2001 and Gyselen 2002; on Xusraw's reforms see the recent Gariboldi 2006.

[107] Schindel 2004, 3/1, pp. 128-178.

[108] Gyselen 1989a, p. 3, refers to MHD 93, 4-9.

[109] Gyselen 1989b, pp. 521-522.

BBA (*dar* = the Court), officially working since Wahrām IV.[110]

This articulate system of mints is evidence of a high level of organization and of the centralization of the Sasanian Empire. The imperial administration, as underlined by Gyselen, was operating mainly on three hierarchic levels: the region (*kust*), the province (*šahr*), and the canton (*rōstāg* or *tāsōg*). But the provinces were the real vital centre of the empire; they were governed by a *šahrab* or even by a *mowbed*, a Mazdean priest, meaning that the Zoroastrian clergy was a fundamental part of the State bureaucracy, to such an important level to be the *mowh*, "Office of the Magi", the closest authority to rely on in the local or cantonal area. The most important offices concerning the regions that can be called super-*šahr* were assigned to an *āmārgar* (administrator) or to a *framādār* (commander),[111] that probably were selected among the aristocracy or members of the Court.

Hereunder is the recapitulation of the administrative hierarchy, pictured in a pyramidal table:

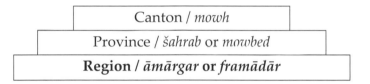

| Canton / *mowh* |
| Province / *šahrab* or *mowbed* |
| **Region / *āmārgar* or *framādār*** |

Göbl has noticed that, especially during the fifth century A.D., sometimes the coins issued by different mints, even very far from one another, represent portraits stylistically similar, so it can be deduced that some central mints supplied the engravers with the dies already prepared,

---

[110] Schindel 2004, 3/1, p. 132.

[111] They could also be *wāspuhragān framādārs*, "special/courtier commanders": Gyselen 2002, pp. 77-78; 119-120.

and it seems that only the legends and the dates had to be added on it. Old dies were rarely reused, but the re-cutting of a reverse die was sometimes practised as we can see, for example, on the reverse of our coin n. 27, which is a drachm of Wahrām IV with the mint-mark KL (Kirmān) engraved on the left of the altar, while on the right side is visible an erased letter. The coin legends, that had become very long by that time, were drastically abbreviated starting from the fiscal and economic reform of Kawād I and Xusraw I since the collection of money from taxes that previously were paid mostly in kind, probably called for coins to be more easily produced and to be read. Perhaps the obverse-dies of the coins were coming from the official centres that were in close contact with the royal authorities in charge of the coinage, such as the *wāstaryōšān sālār*, "the chief of husbandmen", like a Minister of Finance, similar to the Roman *rationalis*, whereas the reverse-dies, that become consumed very easily being hardly hit with the hammer during the striking, were more likely made *in loco* (moreover, they had to be changed at least once in a year due to the date).

The quantities of coins to be struck were fixed in advance by the authorities and, for example, the historian Tabarī[112] (tenth century), reports that in the thirteenth and thirtieth year of Xusraw II, new dies were struck with the aim to double the number of coins in the royal treasury. During critical moments either the conquering wars of Šābuhr II or the disastrous military campaigns of Pērōz against the Hephthalites (that imitated the Sasanian coins), to whom the Sasanians had to pay heavy tributes, or for financing the wars against the Byzantines, the quantity of the coinage increased very much. As it happened in ancient times, besides the exploitation of the mines, in order

---

[112] Nöldeke 1879, pp. 376-377; Bosworth 1999, pp. 392-394.

to cope with these needs, it was possible to melt old or foreign coins, sometimes coming from war spoils; this fact can explain the relative rarity of the coins of the first Sasanian kings. Rather than this, the Arabs continued to use Sasanian silver coins for some centuries onward without re-melting them as testified from the hoards.

The circulation of the Sasanian coins, particularly as regards the silver drachms (not considering the copper coins because they were used for local purchases, as previously explained), was quite amazing, as it was spread all over a vast area, including even Sweden,[113] China, India, and Sri Lanka.[114] Only an accurate study of hoards and sporadic coin finds will outline precisely the borders of the Sasanian coins circulation. For example, F. Thierry[115] has dedicated his study to some Sasanian coins found in China, analysing sixty different places including funerary, religious deposits, and proper hoards. His research has modified the consolidated idea of coin circulation from West to East only due to the trade of silk demonstrating that, for the Chinese, the foreign coins were just a reserve of precious material, without any link to monetary circulation. In fact, the Chinese used only copper coins, that obviously were not accepted by Western traders, who were instead interested in wheat, spices, and valuable fabrics in exchange of pharmacopoeia products, noble metals, transparent glass, and precious stones. Therefore, the Sasanian drachms were considered just like reserve treasures, mainly imported by the Hephthalites after the wars against Pērōz. So far the Chinese drachms were not properly included in their monetary system. On the contrary, for what concerns Central Asia, the Sasanian coins seemed to be well inte-

---

[113] Malek 1993, pp. 247-248.
[114] Bopearachchi 1993.
[115] Thierry 1993 and Thierry 1999.

grated in the monetary circulation, as proved by the numerous countermarks engraved on the Sasanian coins found in Bactria and in Sogdia. Some Bactrian legal documents testify that silver drachms of Kawād were still used for payments in the Hindukush region, during the seventh century. The Sasanians rarely countermarked the coins with the *frawahr* symbol, which was also the emblem of the royal treasury, but most of the countermarks are dated to the seventh and eighth century and were generally struck by the Arabs, the Iranian Huns and the Sogdians.[116]

Obviously, there are numerous hoards of Sasanian coins in modern Iran, in Iraq, in Russia, and in the Mediterranean area, in Syria or in Jordan,[117] but very often the Sasanian coins are found mixed up with Arab coins (the Arabs used to cut them in order to reach the standard current weight), so this does not help us have a clear idea of the monetary circulation in the Sasanian period. In fact, the Sasanian coins were imported even in Europe, especially in the Central Northern area, but were evidently brought there by traders after some centuries, along with other precious objects only for their intrinsic value. In conclusion, I would like mention the recent "sporadic" finding of a drachm of Wahrām V (420-438 A.D.) in Upper Friuli in Italy[118] that perhaps came there through the flourishing trade activity in Venice.

1.6 Coin legends.

The legends on the Sasanian coins in Middle-Persian or Pahlavi are an innovation, as previously underlined, com-

---

[116] Göbl 1971, p. 56; Nikitin & Roth 1995b; Sims-Williams 1999, pp. 253-255; Schindel 2002; Gyselen 2003.

[117] Malek 1993.

[118] Passera 2002, p. 107, note 123, pl. II, fig. 14. Precisely, the coin was found in the area of the "Canale del Ferro" (Udine), not far from the Tarvisio Pass.

pared to the Parthian coins that used Greek as their official language, while Aramaic was seldom adopted.[119] However, Aramaic was employed on the Parthian coins especially during the second and third centuries A.D., and this fact probably influenced the decision of the Sasanians not to use Greek on the coins anymore although Greek was still well known, at least to those employed in the Court chancellery, as proved by the trilingual inscription of Šābuhr I (*ŠKZ*).[120] So Greek always remained the principal language for communication between the Romans and the Orient;[121] but a strong sense of Sasanian nationalism pushed toward the direction of a political and cultural autonomy that could not leave out of consideration the use of a proper spoken language, perhaps also under the influence of the local tradition of the dynasts of Persis, that always used Aramaic on their coinage and arrogated to themselves the title of King, "MLK" = *šāh*, since Dārēw I (late second century B.C.), which actually was the same title adopted also by Pābag, Ardašīr I's father.[122]

Logically, the legends on the Sasanian coins are inspired by their conception about royalty and religion.[123] The royal titling of Ardašīr I (224-240 A.D.) remained almost unchanged up to Wahrām V (420-438 A.D.) for almost two centuries. The official and complete titulature of Ardašīr is, in transcription: *māzdēsn bay Ardašīr šāhān šāh Ērān kē čihr az yazdān*, "Mazdean Lord Ardašīr King of Kings of the Iranians, whose image/origin is from the Gods".

---

[119] Abgarians & Sellwood 1971.
[120] Huyse 1999.
[121] Rubin 2002.
[122] Alram 1999.
[123] Göbl 1983a, p. 329.

The Middle-Persian legend is read on the coins anti-clockwise. Usually it starts from the upper part on the left of the bust (positioned at 11 o'clock), and very often it is irregularly abbreviated or interrupted in some part. This is sometimes due to lack of space (since the portrait was the first to be engraved on the die and then the mint workers proceeded with the inscription) and sometimes due to the lack of skill of the engravers. Therefore, it is possible to find numerous variants, even curious ones,[124] compared to the canonical coin legends that are the result of an accurate comparison among many specimens. Obviously, better attention was dedicated to the inscriptions on silver drachms and on gold coins. The other denominations can render inscriptions almost illegible, either due to the small dimensions or the poor value of the coins.

As has been already underlined, the titling of Ardašīr establishes a strong and immediate link between the king and religion. He is a Mazdean Lord (*bay*), descendant of the Gods or, more literally, as advanced by Panaino,[125] whose "image" (*čihr*) is that of the Gods (*yazdān*) (see *supra*, for the differentiation of meaning between *bay* and *yazd*).

Concerning the political aspect, it is the first mention of the ethnic: "King of Kings of the Iranians" (*šāhān šāh Ērān*, coming from a genitive plural of Old Persian **aryānām*) appears on Persian coins and, as fully demonstrated by Gnoli's studies,[126] it was the Sasanian cultural and political propaganda itself that sprang the new "idea of Iran" and of an Iranian kingdom, created and supported by Ohrmazd, on the ancestral territory of the *Arya* (likely "Nobles"), creating in this way a real *Ērān-šahr*, a reign of the Aryans.

---

[124] Göbl 1983b, pp. 290-298, pls. I-III.
[125] Panaino 2003a.
[126] Gnoli 1989 and Gnoli 1998.

Šābuhr I, after his important victories over the Romans, proclaimed himself king of *Ērān ud anērān*, "of the Iranians and non-Iranians". He had subjected many people of origin not properly Iranian, living in the so called "outer" Iran such as, for example, the Armenians, the Georgians and the Albans.[127] However, the legend *ud anērān* does not appear on the coins of Šābuhr I, but just on his trilingual inscription even if his successor Ohrmazd I immediately adopted it, confirming that a comparison among the sources is always absolutely necessary.

Yazdgird I (399-420 A.D.) adds to the old titling, also the epithet of *rāmšahr* (*l'mštly*), "who keeps the land at peace" (Cat. n. 29), which was later adopted also by Yazdgird II and Wahrām V, and this probably testifies to a revival of the Kayānid (M.P. *Kayān*) ideology, from whom the Sasanians claimed to descend.[128] So, during the reign of Yazdgird II (438-457 A.D.) the mythic title *kay* "ruler/king" was inserted beside *māzdēsn bay* and the king's name, but the other elements that by that time had become very long, corrupted and almost never written in full, can no longer be observed. Nevertheless, on a few drachms of Pērōz the title of *šāhān šāh* is still present. Walaxš (484-488 A.D.) adopts the additional name *hukay Walaxš*, "the Good King Walaxš". It is not yet clear if the M.P. *hwkl* stands for *hukay* or *hukardār*, "beneficent". During the first reign of Kawād and under Zāmāsp (496-499 A.D.), we can find on the coins only the name of the king, and finally, starting from the sixteenth year (504 A.D.), Kawād also adds the augural

---

[127] Gnoli 1996, pp. 831-861; Piras 2001.

[128] According to the Parthian and Sasanian epic (particularly in the Pahlavi text *Ayādgār ī Zarērān*), *Kay* Wištāsp should have been the first king to adopt the religion of Zoroaster and he fought against the wicked king Arjāsp, who had ordered him to abandon the Zoroastrian faith. See Cereti 2001, pp. 191-192; 200-202; on "Kayānid" ideology see Daryaee 2002a; 2002b.

word 'pzwny, *abzōn* "increase", probably to celebrate the Persian conquering of Amida. Thus a "standardisation" of the legend is reached and almost all the royal titles were removed from the coinage.[129] This formula remained unchanged until Xusraw II, who commonly has on his coins *hwslwb* GDE 'pzwty, "Xusraw (has) increased the *xwarrah* (royal glory)".

Starting from the twelfth regnal year on some drachms of Xusraw II, almost a quarter of the whole production, the word *āfid* ('pd), "good", "excellent", "wonderful" is engraved on the external rim of the obverse, in the second quadrant of the margin, but not all mints followed this directive. However, the meaning of *āfid* is uncertain: for example, it could refer to the good quality of the metal or it

---

[129] It was likely a matter of simplification of the legend on the coins, and also the will to give a more direct message; not to be intended that the kings had renounced their titles. In fact, analysing other primary sources, as the glyptic, we have the confirmation that, in spite of the simplification of the royal titling on the coins, the epithets were usually passed from father to son and accumulated. So, for instance, on a beautiful seal of Pērōz (457-484 A.D.), who has on his coins *māzdēsn bay kay Pērōz*, "Mazdean Lord *Kay* Pērōz", there is a long and complex personal titling and furthermore, we find the titles of his father Yazdgird II and his grandfather Wahrām V, with their titles abbreviated and reduced, compared to the last descendant of the dynasty, in accordance with the Sasanian praxis. Pērōz, in an aulic way, declares himself: *māzdēsn bay rāmšahr kay Pērōz šāhān šāh ī farrox ud xwābar ud kirbakkar kē yazdān nōg xwarrah abzūd ērān ud *anērān kē čihr az yazdān*, "The Mazdean Lord, who keeps the land at peace, *Kay* Pērōz, King of Kings, the fortunate, munificent and beneficent one, in/by whom the new *xwarrah* of the gods has increased, of Iranians and [non-Iranians], whose image/origin is from the gods". We can note, besides the definition of Pērōz as "King of Kings", which is not commonly present on his coinage, an "anticipated" mention of the concept that the king increases the *xwarrah* of the gods, which on the coins generally starts in the second reign of Kawād I. About this exceptional gem, as well as the somewhat problematic interpretation of the inscription, see: Gignoux 2000, pp. 163-166; Skjærvø 2003, pp. 281-286; Schindel 2004, 3/1, pp. 78-79 and 392.

could be an epithet for Xusraw or even a religious invocation. Gurnet has considered all the hypotheses and he is inclined to believe that *āfid* refers to the good quality of the silver, since in analysing the coin hoards a better quality was confirmed, even if only perceptible,[130] of the coins with *āfid*, compared to the ones without it.[131] In fact, Xusraw II could have issued these series of coins in order to pay his troops, on the occasion of the re-establishment of the *xwarrah*, after the elimination of his internal rivals and of his intent to enter again in war against the Byzantines. This was due to Phocas' ascent to the throne in 602 A.D. which occurred exactly in the twelfth year of Xusraw's reign. But I personally think that *āfid*, very likely linked to the new political propaganda of Xusraw (not to forget that he also added two wings on the top of the crown besides the explicit mention of the *xwarrah*), does not necessarily refer to the metal, since there was no reason to declare that a coin was of good quality, as, in ancient times, precious coins were first tested by the bankers and the traders before entering into circulation. Moreover, if the meaning of *āfid* referred to the excellent quality of the coins, no one would have accepted all the other coins that were coined in great quantity. It seems to me that *āfid* could be another invocation with religious shade or a good auspice, as it is also the wish that the *xwarrah* may increase, actually meaning the increase of the king and the power of the empire. Furthermore, it has to be noted that the Arabs reserved the external rim on the obverse of the coins just for the inscription of many religious formulas,[132] such as

---

[130] As admitted also by Gurnet 1999: 113, the weight difference between the two typologies of coins is "de l'ordre de quelques centigrammes".
[131] Gurnet 1994a and Gurnet 1999.
[132] Gyselen 2000b, pp. 91-98.

bismi'llāh, "in the name of Allāh", perhaps to maintain a continuity with the Sasanian coinage.[133]

In conclusion, we have to mention the existence of "special" legends that can be found on emissions that are special too, such as gold coins of Kawād I or Xusraw I,[134] referring to the power and the splendour that the sovereign brings to his kingdom. Such inscriptions do express a propagandistic spirit through political-religious formulas, in particular, on the gold and silver coins of Xusraw II with the supposed representation of the *xwarrah* on the reverse, which we have already mentioned for the frontal posture of the portraits. Recently, Gignoux[135] has interpreted the legend written around the bust surrounded by flames, on some coins of Xusraw II, like: (*Xusraw*) *Ērān abzūd hudēnag*, "(Xusraw) has increased *Ērān*, of good religion", and on other gold coins[136] there is also the legend, recalling the wars against the Byzantines, *Xusraw gēhān abēbīm kardār*, "Xusraw who made the world fearless".

On the reverses of the Sasanian coins, at first there is generally the inscription NWR' ZY "the fire of...", and the name of the king. The heterogram NWR' was finally replaced by Šābuhr III with the Middle-Persian equivalent *'twl* (*ādur*), then it disappeared too due to the gradual introduction of the mint-mark on the right side of the fire-altar, and of the regnal year on the left side, starting from Zāmāsp and the second reign of Kawād I. This important

---

[133] The inscription *āfid* (*'pd*) is engraved on some silver Arab-Sasanian coin too, in the same position as on Xusraw's coins (see Cat. n. 68), but it also appears on some copper coins of the governor 'Ubaydallāh ibn Ziyād of the second half of the seventh century A.D., and this circumstance should spoil the interpretation of Gurnet. See Gyselen 2000b, p. 134, Type 18a.

[134] Mosig & Walburg 1994.

[135] Gyselen 2000a, pp. 309-310; Göbl 1971, pl. 14, ns. 217-218.

[136] Göbl 1971, pl. 14, ns. 220-221.

canonical fixation of the regnal year and the mint-mark on the coins of Kawād I was probably part of a vast plan of administrative and fiscal reforms, implemented by Kawād and Xusraw I. Among them, is included the administrative glyptic, and a complex subdivision of the Sasanian empire in numerous provinces and cantons that will remain almost unvaried up to the first centuries of Arab domination.[137]

---

[137] Daryaee 2003.

CATALOGUE

ARDAŠĪR I (224-240 AD.)
Mint C (Ctesiphon?)
Drachm
Obv: **mzdysn bgy 'rthštr MLKAn MLKA 'yr'n MNW ctry MN yzd'n**
māzdēsn bay Ardašīr šāhān šāh ērān kē čihr az yazdān
Mazdean Lord, Ardašīr, King of Kings of the Iranians, whose image/origin is from the gods.
Bust facing right of Ardašīr I.
Rv: **NWR' ZY 'rthštr**
ādur ī Ardašīr
Fire of Ardašīr
Fire altar.
Bibl.: Alram – Gyselen 2003, Type IIIa/3a,b,c.

1- AR g. 4.43; mm. 26; 3 (pierced and restored coin).
Obv: **[m]zdysn bgy 'rthštr MLKAn MLKA 'yr'n MNW ctry MN yzd'n**
Rv: **NWR' [ZY 'r]thštr**
Brera; N. Inv.: C 1280.

2- AR g. 2.99; mm. 24; 3.
Obv: **mzdysn bgy 'rthštr MLKAn MLKA 'yr'n MNW ctry MN yzd'n**
Rv: **NWR' ZY 'rthštr**
Brera; N. Inv.: Coll. Rolla C s.n.

ŠĀBUHR I (240-272 AD.)
Uncertain Mint
Drachm
Obv: **mzdysn bgy šhpwhry MLKAn MLKA 'yr'n MNW ctry MN yzd'n**
māzdēsn bay Šābuhr šāhān šāh ērān kē čihr az yazdān

69

Mazdean Lord, Šābuhr, King of Kings of the Iranians, whose image/origin is from the gods.
Bust facing right of Šābuhr I.
Rv: **NWR' ZY šhpwhry**
ādur ī Šābuhr
Fire of Šābuhr
Fire altar flanked by two figures.
Bibl.: Alram – Gyselen 2003, Type IIc/1a-b.

3- AR g. 4.06; mm. 25; 2.
Obv: **mzdysn bgy šhpwhry MLKAn MLKA 'yr'n MNW ctry MN yzd'n**
Rv: **NWR' ZY šhpwhry**
Brera; N. Inv.: C 1282.

4- AR g. 4.05; mm. 27; 3.
Obv: **mzdysn bgy šhpwhry MLKAn MLKA 'yr'n MNW ctry MN yzd'n**
Rv: **NWR' ZY šh[pwh]ry**; *frawahr* symbol in field
Brera; N. Inv.: C 1281.

5-AR g. 3.82; mm. 26; 3.
Obv: **mzdysn bgy šh[pwh]ry MLKAn MLKA 'yr'n MNW ctry MN yzd'n**
Rv: **[NWR' ZY šhpwhry]**
Brera; N. Inv.: B 3861.

6- AR g. 3.57; mm. 25; 3.
Obv: **mzdysn bgy šhpwhry MLKAn MLKA 'yr'n MNW ctry MN yzd'n**
Rv: **NWR' ZY šhpwhry**; *frawahr* symbol in field
Brera; N. Inv.: B 3860.

7- AR g. 3.30; mm. 24; 9.
Obv: **mzdysn bgy šhpwhry MLK[An] MLKA 'yr'n MNW ctry MN yzd'n**
Rv: **NWR' ZY [šhpwhry]**
Brera; N. Inv.: C 1283.

WAHRĀM II (276-293 AD.)

Uncertain Mint
Drachm
Obv: **mzdysn bgy wrhr'n MLKAn MLKA 'yr'n W 'nyr'n MNW ctry MN yzd'n**
māzdēsn bay Wahrām šāhān šāh ērān ud anērān kē čihr az yazdān
Mazdean Lord, Wahrām, King of Kings of the Iranians and non-Iranians, whose image/origin is from the gods.
Bust facing right of Wahrām, superposed on a female bust wearing a cap with animal-head, in front of them a small left-facing bust, wearing a cap with animal-head and holding a diadem.
Rv: **NWR' ZY wrhr'n**
ādur ī Wahrām
Fire of Wahrām.
Fire altar flanked by two figures, the left one, wears a winged crown with *korymbos*, the right one, female, holding a wreathed ring; *frawahr* symbol to the left of the flames. Three dots on the altar-shaft.
Bibl.: GÖBL 1971, Type XI/3 (Pl. 5, 71).

8- AR g. 4.35; mm. 28; 3 (corroded coin).
Obv: **mzdysn bgy wrhr'n MLKAn MLKA 'yr'n W 'nyr'n MNW ctry MN yzd'n**
Rv: **NWR' ZY wrhr'n**
Brera; N. Inv.: B 3862.

ŠĀBUHR II (309-379 AD.)
Mint IX (Ctesiphon/Kabul?)
Drachm
Obv: **mzdysn bgy šhpwhry MLKAn MLKA 'yr'n W 'nyr'n (MNW ctry MN yzd'n)**
māzdēsn bay Šābuhr šāhān šāh ērān ud anērān kē čihr az yazdān
Mazdean Lord, Šābuhr, King of Kings of the Iranians and non-Iranians (whose image/origin is from the gods).
Bust facing right of Šābuhr II.
Rv: **NWR' ZY šhpwhry**
ādur ī Šābuhr
Fire of Šābuhr.

Fire altar flanked by two figures; small bust within flames turned right. On altar-shaft: **l'st** (*rāst*) (true).
Bibl.: Schindel 2004, Type Ib1/3a.

9- AR g. 4.30; mm. 22; 3.
Obv: pseudo-legend
Rv: **NWR' (ZY) šhpwhry**; **l'sty**
Brera; N. Inv.: C 1284.

10- AR g. 4.15; mm. 28; 2.
Obv: **mzdysn bgy šhpwhry MLKAn MLKA 'yr'n W 'nyr'n (MNW ctry MN yzd'n)**
Rv: pseudo-legend; **l'st**
Brera; N. Inv.: B 3866.

11- AR g. 4.07; mm. 23; 3 (pierced coin).
Obv: **mzdysn bgy šhpwhry MLKAn MLKA 'yr'n W 'nyr'n (MNW ctry MN yzd'n)**
Rv: **NWR' (ZY) šhpwhry**; **l'st**
Brera; N. Inv.: B 3864.

12- AR g. 4.04; mm. 21; 3.
Obv: **mzdysn bgy šhpwhry MLKAn MLKA 'yr'n W 'nyr'n (MNW ctry MN yzd'n)**
Rv: pseudo-legend
Brera; N. Inv.: C 1285.

13- AR g. 4.02; mm. 23; 3.
Obv: **mzdysn bgy šhpwhry MLKAn MLKA 'yr'n W 'nyr'n (MNW ctry MN yzd'n)**
Rv: pseudo-legend
Brera; N. Inv.: B 3869.

14- AR g. 3.91; mm. 22; 2.
Obv: pseudo-legend
Rv: pseudo-legend
Brera; N. Inv.: B 3871.

15- AR g. 3.84; mm. 25; 3.
Obv: **mzdysn bgy šhpwhry MLKAn MLKA 'yr'n W 'nyr'n (MNW ctry MN yzd'n)**

Rv: no legend
Brera; N. Inv.: B 3867.

16- AR g. 3.79; mm. 24; 3.
Obv: **mzdysn bgy šhpwhry MLKAn MLKA 'yr'n W 'nyr'n
(MNW ctry MN yzd'n)**
Rv: pseudo-legend
Brera; N. Inv.: Coll. Rolla C 1409.

17- AR g. 3.54; mm. 20; 3 (pierced coin)
Obv: pseudo-legend
Rv: pseudo-legend
Brera; N. Inv.: B 3863.

18- AR g. 3.21; mm. 24; 2.
Obv: pseudo-legend
Rv: no legend
Brera; N. Inv.: B 3870.

ŠĀBUHR III (383-388 AD.)
"Western Group"
Drachm
Obv: **mzdysn bgy šhpwhry MLKAn MLKA 'yr'n W 'nyr'n
(MNW ctry MN yzd'n)**
*māzdēsn bay Šābuhr šāhān šāh ērān ud anērān kē čihr az
yazdān*
Mazdean Lord, Šābuhr, King of Kings of the Iranians and non-
Iranians (whose image/origin is from the gods).
Bust facing right of Šābuhr III.
Rv: **'twly (ZY) šhpwhry**
ādur ī Šābuhr
Fire of Šābuhr.
Fire altar flanked by two figures; small bust within flames turned
right. On altar-shaft: **l'st** (*rāst*) (true).
Bibl.: Schindel 2004, Type Ib1/1b.

19- AR g. 3.97; mm. 22; 3.
Obv: **mzdysn bgy šhpwhry MLKAn MLKA 'yr'n W 'nyr'n
(MNW ctry MN yzd'n)**
Rv: illegible

Brera; N. Inv.: B 3865.

20- AR g. 3.89; mm. 25; 2.
Obv: **mzdysn bgy šhpwhry MLKAn MLKA 'yr'n W 'nyr'n
(MNW ctry MN yzd'n)**
Rv: pseudo-legend
Brera; N. Inv.: B 3874.

21- AR g. 3.85; mm. 22; 3.
Obv: pseudo-legend
Rv: pseudo-legend
Brera; N. Inv.: B 3872.

22- AR g. 3.79; mm. 24; 3.
Obv: **mzdysn bgy šhpwhry MLKAn MLKA 'yr'n W 'nyr'n
(MNW ctry MN yzd'n)**
Rv: pseudo-legend
Brera; N. Inv.: B 3876.

WAHRĀM IV (388-399 AD.)
Mint DAL
Drachm
Obv: **mzdysn bgy wlhl'n MLKAn MLKA ('yr'n W 'nyr'n
MNW ctry MN yzd'n)**
*māzdēsn bay Wahrām šāhān šāh ērān ud anērān kē čihr az
yazdān*
Mazdean Lord, Wahrām, King of Kings of the Iranians and non-
Iranians (whose image/origin is from the gods).
Bust facing right of Wahrām IV.
Rv: **'twly wlhl'n**
ādur; *Wahrām*
Fire; Wahrām.
Fire altar flanked by two figures; small bust on the top of the
altar turned right.
To the left of the bust: **d'l**.
Bibl.: Schindel 2004, Type Ia1/2a.

23- AR g. 4.06; mm. 26; 9.
Obv: **mzdysn bgy wlhl'n MLKAn MLKA ('yr'n W 'nyr'n
MNW ctry MN yzd'n)**

Rv: pseudo-legend; to the left of the bust **d'l**.
Brera; N. Inv.: B 3873.

24- AR g. 4.01; mm. 23; 3 (pierced coin).
Obv: **mzdysn bgy wlhl'n MLKAn MLKA ('yr'n W 'nyr'n MNW ctry MN yzd'n)**
Rv: no legend; to the right of the altar '(a).
Brera; N. Inv.: B 3875.

25- AR g. 3.85; mm. 25; 3.
Obv: **mzdysn bgy wlhl'n MLKAn MLKA ('yr'n W 'nyr'n MNW ctry MN yzd'n)**
Rv: no legend
Brera; N. Inv.: B 3868.

26- AR g. 3.67; mm. 23; 3.
Obv: pseudo-legend
Rv: no legend (Type 2b)
Brera; N. Inv.: Coll. Rolla C 1410.

WAHRĀM IV (388-399 AD.)
Mint KL
Drachm
Obv: **mzdysn bgy wlhl'n ZY MLKAn MLKA ('yr'n W 'nyr'n MNW ctry MN yzd'n)**
māzdēsn bay Wahrām ī šāhān šāh ērān ud anērān kē čihr az yazdān
Mazdean Lord, Wahrām, of the King of Kings of the Iranians and non-Iranians (whose image/origin is from the gods).
Bust facing right of Wahrām IV.
Rv: **'twly wlhl'n**
ādur Wahrām
Fire; Wahrām.
Fire altar flanked by two figures; to the left of the flames: **kl**. On altar-shaft: **l'st** (*rāst*) (true).
Bibl.: Schindel 2004, Type Ia1/3.

27- AR g. 4.15; mm. 24; 3.
Obv: **mzdysn bgy wlhl'n ZY MLKAn MLKA ('yr'n W 'nyr'n MNW ctry MN yzd'n)**

Rv: **'twly wlhl'n**; to the left of the flames **kl**; to the right erased letter; **l'st** on altar-shaft.
Brera; N. Inv.: B 3877.
(Schindel 2004, Tafel 39, A41 – this same coin)

28- AR g. 3.91; mm. 22; 1.
Mint AS
Obv: **mzdysn bgy wlhl'n ZY MLKAn MLKA ('yr'n W 'nyr'n MNW ctry MN yzd'n)**
Rv: **'twly wlhl'n**; to the left of the flames **as**; **[l'st]** on altar-shaft.
Brera; N. Inv.: B 3878.

YAZDGIRD I (399-420 AD.)
Mint AWH
Drachm
Obv: **mzdysn bgy l'mštly yzdklty MLKAn MLKA**
māzdēsn bay rāmšahr Yazdgird šāhān šāh
Mazdean Lord Yazdgird, who keeps the land at peace, King of Kings.
Bust facing right of Yazdgird I.
Rv: no legend.
Fire altar flanked by two figures; to the left of the altar: **h**; on altar-shaft: **l'st** (*rāst*) (true); to the right **'w**. Over the flames, three crescents and two dots.
Bibl.: Schindel 2004, Type Ia1/1a, var.6.

29- AR g. 3.37; mm. 26; 3.
Obv: **mzdysn bgy l'mštly yzdklty MLKAn MLKA**
Rv: to the left of the altar: **h**; on altar-shaft: **l'st** (*rāst*) (true); to the right **'w**. Over the flames, three crescents and two dots.
Brera; N. Inv.: C 1286.

WAHRĀM V (420-438 AD.)
Mint AY
Drachm
Obv: **wlhl'n MLKAn MLKA**
Wahrām šāhān šāh
Wahrām King of Kings.
Bust facing right of Wahrām V.

Rv: **wlhl'n**
Wahrām
Fire altar flanked by two figures; king's bust on altar; to the left
wlhl'n; to the right **'y**.
Bibl.: Schindel 2004, Type Ib2/2.

30- AR g. 3.93; mm. 29; 3.
Obv: **wlhl'n MLKAn MLKA**
Rv: to the left **wlhl'n**; to the right **'y**.
Brera; N. Inv.: Coll. Rolla C s. n.

YAZDGIRD II (438-457 AD.)
Uncertain Mint
Drachm
Obv: **mzdysn bgy kdy yzdklty**
māzdēsn bay kay Yazdgird
Mazdean Lord Kay Yazdgird.
Bust facing right of Yazdgird II.
Rv: **nwky yzdklty**
nōg Yazdgird
The new (fire of) Yazdgird.
Fire altar flanked by two figures; to the right **nwky**; to the left
yzdklty.
Bibl.: Schindel 2004, Type Ib1/2b.

31- AR g. 3.91; mm. 32; 3 (pierced coin).
Obv: **mzdysn bgy kdy yzdklty**
Rv: to the right **nwky**; to the left **yzdklty**.
Brera; N. Inv.: B 3880.

32- AR g. 3.73; mm. 28; 2 (pierced coin).
Obv: **mzdysn bgy kdy yzdklty**
Rv: to the right **nwky**; to the left **yzdklty**.
Brera; N. Inv.: B 3879.
PĒRŌZ (457-484 AD.)
Mint AY
Drachm
Obv: **mzdysn bgy kdy pylwcy**
māzdēsn bay kay Pērōz
Mazdean Lord Kay Pērōz.

Bust facing right of Pērōz.
Rv: to the left **pylwcy**; to the right **'y.**
Pērōz.
Fire altar flanked by two figures.
Bibl.: Schindel 2004, Type IIIb/1c.

33- AR g. 4.11; mm. 29; 3.
Obv: **mzdysn bgy kdy pylwcy**
Rv: to the left **pylwcy**; to the right **'y.**
Brera; N. Inv.: Coll. Rolla C 1412.

34- AR g. 3.98; mm. 30; 3 (pierced coin)
Mint KL
Obv: **mzdysn bgy kdy pylwcy**
Rv: to the left **pylwcy**; to the right **kl.**
Brera; N. Inv.: B 3881.

35- AR g. 3.96; mm. 29; 3.
Obv: **[mzdysn bgy kdy pylwcy]**
Rv: to the left **pylwcy**; mint mark illegible.
Brera; N. Inv.: B 3883.

36- AR g. 3.86; mm. 27; 2 (pierced coin)
Mint DA
Obv: **mzdysn bgy kdy pylwcy**
Rv: to the left **pylwcy**; to the right **d'.**
Brera; N. Inv.: B 3882.

WALAXŠ (484-488 AD.)
Mint LD
Drachm
Obv: **hwkd wld'š**
hukay Walaxš
The Good King Walaxš.
Bust facing right of Walaxš; flame on left shoulder.
Rv: to the left **wld'š**; to the right **[l]d.**
Walaxš.
Fire altar flanked by two figures; king's bust on altar.
Bibl.: Schindel 2004, Type Ib/1b.

37- AR g. 4.11; mm. 28; 1.
Obv: **hwkd wld'š**
Rv: to the left **wld'š**; to the right **[l]d**.
Brera; N. Inv.: Coll. Rolla C 1413.

38- AR g. 4.10; mm. 28; 3.
Mint LD
Obv: **hwkd wld'š**
Rv: to the left **[wld'š]**; to the right **ld**.
Brera; N. Inv.: Coll. Rolla C 1414.

KAWĀD I (First reign: 488-496 AD.)
Mint KL
Drachm
Obv: **kw't**, to the right.
Kawād
Bust facing right of Kawād I.
Rv: **kw't**, to the left; to the right **kl**.
Kawād
Fire altar flanked by two figures.
Bibl.: Schindel 2004, Type I/1.

39- AR g. 4.08; mm. 29; 2.
Obv: **kw't**, to the right.
Rv: **[kw't]**, to the left; to the right **kl**.
Brera; N. Inv.: Coll. Rolla C 1415.

KAWĀD I (Second reign: 499-531 AD.)
Year 15
Mint LYW
Drachm
Obv: **kw't**, to the right.
Kawād
Kawād.
Bust facing right of Kawād I.
Rv: **p(')ncdh**, to the left; to the right **lyw**.
pānzdah (15)
Fire altar flanked by two figures.
Bibl.: Schindel 2004, Type Ib/1a.

40- AR g. 3.82; mm. 30; 3.
Obv: **kw't**, to the right.
Rv: **p(')ncdh**, to the left; to the right **lyw**.
Brera; N. Inv.: B 3884.

KAWĀD I (Second reign: 499-531 AD.)
Year 38
Mint AS
Drachm
Obv: **kw't 'pzwny**; to the right.
Kawād abzōn
Kawād; increase.
Bust facing right of Kawād I.
Rv: **hštsy(h)**, to the left; to the right, **'s**.
haštsīh (38)
Fire altar flanked by two figures.
Bibl.: Schindel 2004, Type Ic/1b.

41- AR g. 3.98; mm. 30; 3 (pierced coin).
Obv: **kw't 'pzwny**; to the right.
Rv: **hšt[sy(h)]**, to the left; to the right, **'s**.
Brera; N. Inv.: B 3886.

XUSRAW I (531-579 AD.)
Year 23
Mint ART
Drachm
Obv: **hwslwd 'pzwn**
Xusraw abzōn
Xusraw; increase.
Bust facing right of Xusraw I.
Rv: **sycwysty**, to the left; to the right, **'rt**.
sēzwīst (23)
Fire altar flanked by two figures.
Bibl.: Göbl 1971, Type II/2.

42- AR g. 4.12; mm. 29; 2.
Obv: **hwslwd 'pzwn**
Rv: **sycwysty**, to the left; to the right, **'rt**.
Brera; N. Inv.: Coll. Rolla C 1416.

43- AR g. 4.08; mm. 32; 3.
Year 44
Mint LD
Obv: **hwslwd 'pzwn**
Rv: **chlchl**, to the left; to the right, **ld.**
čahārčehel (44)
Brera; N. Inv.: Coll. Rolla C 1418.

44- AR g. 4.08; mm. 31; 3.
Year 36
Mint AYLAN
Obv: **hwslwd 'pzwn**
Rv: **ššsy,** to the left; to the right, **'yl'n.**
šāssīh (36)
Brera; N. Inv.: Coll. Rolla C 1417.

OHRMAZD IV (579-590 AD.)
Year 10
Mint AY
Drachm
Obv: **'whlmzd 'pzwn**
Ohrmazd abzōn
Ohrmazd; increase.
Bust facing right of Ohrmazd IV.
Rv: **'SL'**, to the left; to the right, **'y.**
dah (10)
Fire altar flanked by two figures.
Bibl.: Göbl 1971, Type I/1.

45- AR g. 4.17; mm. 33; 9.
Obv: **'whlmzd 'pzwn**
Rv: **'SL'**, to the left; to the right, **'y.**
Brera; N. Inv.: C 1288.

46- AR g. 4.11; mm. 32; 4.
Year 7
Mint AW
Obv: **'whlmzd 'pzwn**
Rv: **ŠB'**, to the left; to the right, **'w.**

haft (7)
Brera; N. Inv.: C 1287.

47- AR g. 4.09; mm. 34; 3.
Year 7
Mint YZ
Obv: **'whlmzd 'pzwn**
Rv: **ŠB'**, to the left; to the right, **yz.**
haft (7)
Brera; N. Inv.: B 3888.

48- AR g. 4.09; mm. 32; 3.
Year 8
Mint NAL
Obv: **'whlmzd 'pzwn**
Rv: **T[W]MN'**, to the left; to the right, **n'l.**
hašt (8)
Brera; N. Inv.: C 1291.

49- AR g. 3.59; mm. 30; 3.
Year 9
Mint AW
Obv: **'whlmzd 'pzwn**
Rv: **TŠ'**, to the left; to the right, **'w.**
nō (9)
Brera; N. Inv.: Coll. Rolla C 1419.

50- AR g. 3.31; mm. 30; 3.
Year 6
Mint YZ
Obv: **'whlmzd 'pzwn**
Rv: **ŠT'**, to the left; to the right, **yz.**
šaš (6)
Brera; N. Inv.: C 1289.

51- AR g. 3.17; mm. 31; 9.
Year 12
Mint YZ
Obv: **'whlmzd 'pzwn**
Rv: **dw'cdh**, to the left; to the right, **yz.**

dwāzdah (12)
Brera; N. Inv.: C 1290.

XUSRAW II (590/91- 628 AD.)
Year 9
Mint GD
Drachm
Obv: **hwslwb GDE 'pzwty**
Xusraw xwarrah abzūd
Xusraw (has) increased the royal glory.
Bust facing right of Xusraw II.
Rv: **TŠ'**, to the left; to the right, **gd.**
nō (9)
Fire altar flanked by two figures.
Bibl.: Göbl 1971, Type II/3.

52- AR g. 4.02; mm. 31; 2.
Obv: **hwslwb GDE 'pzwn**
Rv: **TŠ'**, to the left; to the right, **gd.**
Brera; N. Inv.: Coll. Rolla C 1420.

53- AR g. 4.00; mm. 31; 3.
Year 2
Mint AW
Obv: **hwslwb GDE 'pzwty**
Rv: **TLYN**, to the left; to the right, **aw.**
dō (2)
Brera; N. Inv.: B 3885.

54- AR g. 3.99; mm. 32; 3.
Mint AW
Obv: **hwslwb [GDE 'pzwty]**
Rv: year illegible; to the right, **aw.**
Brera; N. Inv.: B 3893.

55- AR g. 3.93; mm. 33; 9.
Year 9
Obv: **hwslwb GDE 'pzwty**
Rv: **TŠ'**, to the left; illegible mint.
nō (9)

Brera; N. Inv.: B 3889.

56- AR g. 3.91; mm. 31; 3.
Mint LYW
Obv: **hwslwb GDE 'pzwty**
Rv: year illegible; to the right, **lyw.**
Brera; N. Inv.: C 1296.

57- AR g. 3.87; mm. 30; 3.
Year 4
Mint NY
Obv: **[hwslwb GDE 'pzwty]**
Rv: **'LB'**, to the left; to the right, **ny.**
čahār (4)
Brera; N. Inv.: B 3892.

58- AR g. 3.82; mm. 32; 3 (pierced coin).
Obv: **hwslwb GDE 'pzwty**
Rv: year illegible; to the right, [.]**d.**
Brera; N. Inv.: C 1294.

59- AR g. 3.79; mm. 31; 4 (pierced coin).
Year 6
Mint DA
Obv: **hwslwb GDE ['pzwty]**
Rv: **ŠT'**, to the left; to the right, **d'.**
šaš (6)
Brera; N. Inv.: B 3891.

60- AR g. 3.75; mm. 30; 3.
Year 3
Mint BYŠ
Obv: **hwslwb GDE 'pzwty**
Rv: **TLT'**, to the left; to the right, **byš.**
sē (3)
Brera; N. Inv.: C 1295.

61- AR g. 3.38; mm. 30; 3.
Year 27
Mint DA

Obv: **hwslwb GDE 'pzwty**
Rv: **hptwyst**, to the left; to the right, **d'**.
haftwīst (27)
Brera; N. Inv.: C 1292.

62- AR g. 2.95; mm. 29; 3.
Year 37
Mint ART
Obv: **hwslwb GDE 'pzwty**
Rv: **hptsyh**, to the left; to the right, **'rt**.
haftsīh (37)
Brera; N. Inv.: B 3890.

63- AR g. 2.91; mm. 28; 3.
Year 11
Mint BBA
Obv: **hwslwb GDE 'pzwty**
Rv: **y'cdh**, to the left; to the right, **bb'**.
yāzdah (11)
Brera; N. Inv.: C 1298.

64- AR g. 2.68; mm. 27; 3.
Year 6
Mint WYHC
Obv: **hwslwb GDE 'pzwty**
Rv: **ŠT'**, to the left; to the right, **wyhc**.
šaš (6)
Brera; N. Inv.: C 1293.

65- AR g. 2.60; mm. 26; 3.
Year 34
Mint AHM
Obv: **hwslwb GDE 'pzwty**
Rv: **chl[syh]**, to the left; to the right, **'hm**.
čahārsīh (34)
Brera; N. Inv.: C 1297.

66- AR g. 2.12; mm. 25; 3 (pierced and broken coin)
Mint GD
Obv: **hwslwb [GDE 'pzwty]**

Rv: year illegible; to the right, **gd.**
Brera; N. Inv.: B 3894.

ARAB-SASANIAN COINS

al-Muhallab ibn Abī Ṭufrā (694-698 AD.)
Year 76
Mint BYŠ
Drachm
Obv: **mwh'lp y 'bwcwpr'n**, to the right; **GDE 'pzwt**, to the left; in the second quadrant of the margin, **bsm'llh** (*bismi'llāh*, "in the name of Allāh"); in the third quadrant of the margin, **mw** (for **mwh'lp**).
Bust facing right of al-Muhallab ibn Abī Ṭufrā.
Rv: **šš'pt't**, to the left; to the right, **byš.**
šašhaftād (76)
Fire altar flanked by two figures.
Bibl.: Gaube 1973, Tafel 5, n. 60 (similar).

67- AR g. 3.37; mm. 31; 3.
Obv: **mwh'lp y 'bwcwpr'n**, to the right; **GDE 'pzwt**, to the left; in the second quadrant of the margin, **bsm'llh**; in the third quadrant of the margin, **mw.**
Rv: **šš'pt't**, to the left; to the right, **byš.**
Brera; N. Inv.: B 3887.

'Umar ibn al-'Alā (771-780 AD.)
Year 127
Ṭabaristān
Half-drachm
Obv: **GDE 'pzwty**, to the left; to the right, **'wmr**; in the second quadrant of the margin, **'pd** (*afīd*, "good").
Bust facing right of 'Umar ibn al-'Alā.
Rv: **hptwystst**, to the left; to the right, **tpwlst'n.**
haftwīstsad (127)
Fire altar flanked by two figures.
Bibl.: Gaube 1973, Tafel 11, n. 142; Malek 1996, p. 182, ns. 29-41.

68- AR g. 1.94; mm. 25; 11.

Obv: **GDE 'pzwty**, to the left; to the right, **'wmr**; in the second quadrant of the margin, **'pd**.
Rv: **hptwystst**, to the left; to the right, **tpwlst'n**.
Brera; N. Inv.: B 3895.

MODERN CAST FORGERY

ARDAŠĪR I (224-240 AD.)
Similar to ns. 1-2

69- AR g. 4.46; mm. 24; 3.
Obv: **mzdysn bgy 'rthštr MLKAn MLKA 'yr'n MNW ctry MN yzd'n**
Rv: **NWR' ZY 'rthštr**
Brera; N. Inv.: C 1279.

SASANIAN MINTS

AHM (Hamadān) = 65
ART (Ardašīr-xwarrah) = 42, 62
AS (Asōrestān ?) = 28, 41
AW, AWH (Ohrmazd-Ardašīr) = 29, 46, 49, 53, 54
AY (Ērān-xwarrah-Šābuhr) = 30, 33, 45
AYLAN (Ērān-āsān-kar-Kawād) = 44
BBA (dar, "the Court") = 63
BYŠ (Bīšābuhr) = 60
DA, DAL (Dārābgird) = 23, 36, 59, 61
GD (Gay) = 52, 66
KL (Kirmān) = 27, 34, 39
LD (Ray) = 37, 38, 43
LYW (Rew-Ardašīr) = 40, 56
NAL (Nārmašīr ?) = 48
NY (Nēhāwand) = 57
WYHC (Weh-az-Amid-Kawād) = 64
YZ (Yazd) = 47, 50, 51

ARAB-SASANIAN MINTS

BYŠ (Bīšābuhr) = 67
TPWLST'N (Ṭabaristān) = 68

PLATES

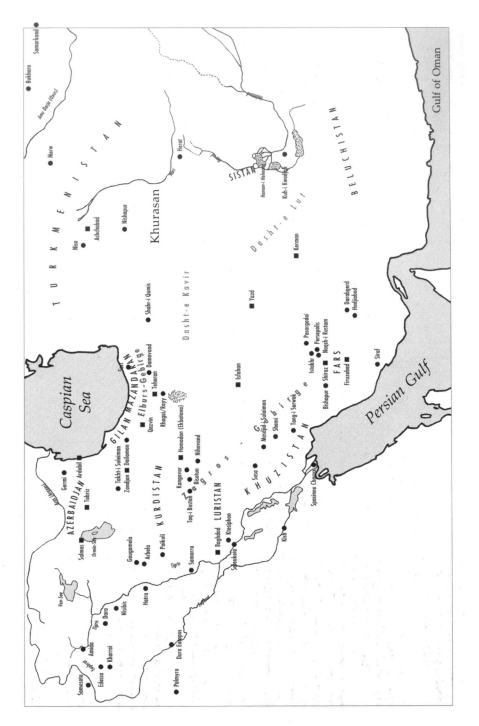

Fig. 1: Map of Ancient Iran (Alram 2000, p. 330)

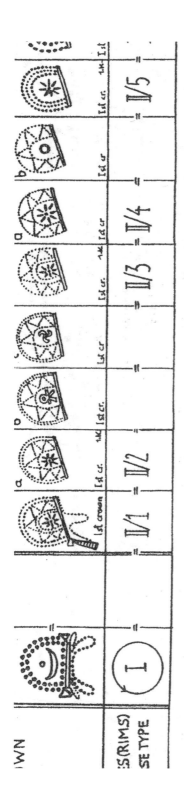

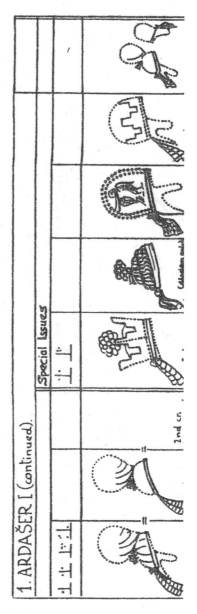

Fig. 2: Typology of Ardašīr Crowns (Göbl 1971, Table 1)

Fig. 3: Relief of Naqš-i Rustam (Alram 2000, p. 268)

Fig. 4: Relief of Firuzabad (Ghirshman 1962, p. 125)

Fig. 5: Relief of Bishapur (Alram 2000, p. 271)

Figure 6: Statue of Šābuhr I at Bishapur

Fig. 7: Cameo with Šābuhr I and Valerianus, Paris Bibliothèque
nationale (Ghirshman 1962, p. 152)

Fig. 8: Sasanian Silver Plate, National Museum of Tehran
(Alram 2000, p. 286)

Fig. 9: Plaster bust of Šābuhr II, National Museum of Tehran
(Alram 2000, p. 279)

1   2   3

4   5

6

7

8

9

10

11 12 13

14 15

16 17 18

19 20

21

22

23   24   25

26   27

28   29   30

31   32

33   34   35

36   37

38   39   40

41   42

43 44 45

46 47

48　　　　　　　49　　　　　　　50

51　　　　　　　52

53 54 55

56 57

58   59   60

61   62

63

64

65

66

67

68

69

Bibliography

Abgarians, M.T. & Sellwood D.G. (1971), A Hoard of Early Parthian Drachms, *The Numismatic Chronicle* 11, pp. 103-134, Pls. 20-23.

Album S., Bates M. & Floor W. (1993), Coins and Coinage. The Sasanians (224-ca.650), *Encyclopaedia Iranica*, VI/1, Costa Mesa, CA, pp. 16-23.

Alram, M. (1986), *Nomina Propria Iranica in Nummis*. Iranisches Personennamenbuch. Band IV, Wien.

_____. (1999), The Beginning of Sasanian Coinage, *Bulletin of the Asia Institute* 13, pp. 67-76.

_____. (2000), Die Kunst im Sasanidenstaat, *7000 Jahre persische Kunst. Meisterwerke aus dem Iranischen Nationalmuseum in Tehran*, hrsg. von Wilfried Seipel, Milano-Wien, pp. 263-295.

_____. (2004), The History of the Silk Road as Reflected in Coins, *Parthica* 6, pp. 47-68.

Alram, M. & Gyselen R. (2003), *Sylloge Nummorum Sasanidarum: Paris – Berlin – Wien*. Band 1: *Ardashir I – Shapur I*, Wien.

Alram, M. & Klimburg Salter (eds.) (1999), *Coins, Art, and Chronology: Essays on the pre-Islamic History of the Indo-Iranian Borderlands*, Wien.

Badiyi, B. (2004), Sasanian Coinage. An Analysis of Base Metal and AE Fractions in the Context of Sasanian Economy in the Fifth and Sixth Century AD. Part I: Varhran V to Khusru I, Costa Mesa (forthcoming).

Bastien, P. (1992-1994), *Le buste monétaire des empereurs romains*, Numismatique Romaine 19, Wetteren.

111

Bates, M. (1987), Arab-Sasanian Coins, *Encyclopaedia Iranica*, II/3, Costa Mesa, pp. 225-229.

Bigwood, J.M. (2004), Queen Mousa, Mother and Wife (?) of King Phraatakes of Parthia: a Re-evaluation of the Evidence, *Mouseion* Vol. 4, pp. 35-70.

Bivar, A.D.H. (1991), The Ideogram for "Staters" in Pahlavi, *Corolla Iranica: Papers in Honour of Prof. Dr. David Neil MacKenzie*, Frankfurt am Main, pp. 3-14.

Bopearachchi, O. (1993), La circulation des monnaies d'origine étrangère dans l'antique Sri Lanka, *Circulation des monnaies, des marchandises et des biens*, éd. R. Gyselen, Res Orientales V, Bures-sur-Yvette, pp. 63-87.

Bosworth, C.E. (1999), *The History of al-Ṭabarī, Vol. V, The Sāsānids, the Byzantines, the Lakhmids, and Yemen*, ed. E. Yar-Shater, New York.

Bravar G. (1982), Monete dell'antica Persia da una collezione triestina, *Atti dei Civici Musei di Storia ed Arte di Trieste* 12-13, pp. 57-83.

Burnett, A., Amandry M. & Ripollès P.P. (1992), *Roman Provincial Coinage. Vol. I. From the Death of Caesar to the Death of Vitellius* (44 BC-AD 69), London – Paris.

Callieri, P. (1998), A proposito di un'iconografia monetale dei dinasti del Fārs post-achemenide, *Ocnus. Quaderni della Scuola di Specializzazione in Archeologia di Bologna* 6, pp. 25-38.

Carile, A. (2000), Le insegne del potere a Bisanzio, *La corona e i simboli del potere*, Rimini, pp. 65-124.

Cereti, C.G. (1995-1997), Primary Sources for the History of Inner and Outer Iran in the Sasanian Period, *Archivum Eurasiae Medii Aevi IX*, pp. 17-69.

_____. (2001), *La letteratura pahlavi*, Milano.

_____. (2004), Some Notes on the Sasanian Coinage of Esfahān and a Few Mint Signatures, *Convegno Internazi-*

onale: La Persia e Bisanzio, Atti dei Convegni Lincei 201, Roma, pp. 309-326.

Choksy, J.K. (1988), Sacral Kingship in Sasanian Iran, *Bulletin of the Asia Institute* 2, pp. 35-52.

Choksy, J.K. (1989), A Sāsānian Monarch, his Queen, Crown Prince, and Deities: the Coinage of Wahrām II, *American Journal of Numismatics* 1, pp. 117-135 (Pl. 10).

Christensen, A. (1925), *Le règne du Roi Kawādh I et le communisme mazdakite,* København.

_____. (1944), *L'Iran sous les Sassanides.* Copenhagen².

Crawford, M.H. (1974), *Roman Republican Coinage,* 2 Vols., Cambridge.

Cribb, J. (1990), Numismatic Evidence for Kushano-Sasanian Chronology, *Studia Iranica* 19, pp. 151-193 (Pls. I-VIII).

Crone, P. (1991), Kavād's Heresy and Mazdak's Revolt, *Iran* 29, pp. 21-42.

Curiel R. & Gyselen R. (1987), Monnaies des fouilles de Bīshāpūr, *Studia Iranica* 16, pp. 7-43 (Pls. I-IV).

Curtis, V.S. (1999), Some Observations on Coins of Peroz and Kavad I, *Coins, Art and Chronology. Essays on the Pre-Islamic History of the Indo-Iranian Borderlands,* Michael Alram & Deborah E. Klimburg-Salter eds., Wien, pp. 303-313.

Daryaee, T. (1997), The Use of Religio-Political Propaganda on the coinage of Xusrō II, *Journal of the American Numismatic Society* Vol. 9, pp. 41-53.

_____. (1998), Sasanian Persia (ca. 224-651 C.E.), *Iranian Studies* 31, 3-4, pp. 431-461.

_____. (1999a), Sources for the Economic History of Late Sāsānian Fārs, *Matériaux pour l'histoire économique du monde iranien,* textes réunis par R. Gyselen R. et M. Szuppe, Cahier de Studia Iranica 21, Paris, pp. 131-148.

_____. (1999b), The Coinage of Queen Bōrān and Its Significance for Late Sāsānian Imperial Ideology, *Bulletin of the Asia Institute* 13, pp. 77-82.

_____. (2002a), Memory and History: The Construction of the Past in Late Antique Persia, *Nāme-ye Irān-e Bāstān* 1, No. 2, pp. 1-14.

_____. (2002b), History, Epic, and Numismatics: on the Title of Yazdgerd I (*Rāmšahr*), *American Journal of Numismatics* 14, pp. 89-95.

_____. (2002c), *Šahrestānīhā ī Ērānšahr. A Middle Persian Text on Late Antique Geography, Epic and History.* With English and Persian Translations and Commentary, Costa Mesa, CA.

_____. (2003), The Effect of the Arab Muslim Conquest on the Administrative Division of Sasanian Persis/Fars, *Iran* 41, 193-204.

De Bruijn E. & Dudley D. (1995), The Humeima Hoard: Byzantine and Sasanian Coins and Jewelry from Southern Jordan, *American Journal of Archaeology* 99, pp. 683-697.

De Morgan, J. (1936), *Manuel de numismatique orientale*, Paris.

Erdmann, K. (1951), Die Entwicklung der sāsānidischen Krone, *Ars Islamica* 15/16, pp. 87-123.

Fiorani Piacentini, V. (1992), *Merchants – Merchandise and Military Power in the Persian Gulf*, Atti della Accademia Nazionale dei Lincei, Memorie (Serie IX, III, 2), Roma.

Frye, R.N. (1972), Gestures of Deference to Royalty in Ancient Iran, *Iranica Antiqua* 9, pp. 102-107.

_____. (1973), *Sasanian Remains from Qasr-i Abu Nasr. Seals, Sealings, and Coins*, Cambridge, MA.

_____. (1984), *The History of Ancient Iran*, München.

_____. (1996), Commerce III. In the Parthian and Sasanian Periods, *Encyclopaedia Iranica* VI/1, Costa Mesa, CA, pp. 61-64.

Gall, H. v. (1990), *Das Reiterkampfbild in der iranischen und iranisch beeinflussten Kunst*, Berlin.

Gariboldi, A. (2000), Simboli e ideologia del potere in età romana, *La corona e i simboli del potere*, Rimini, pp. 31-63.

_____. (2003), *La monetazione sasanide nelle Civiche Raccolte Numismatiche di Milano*, Milano.

_____. (2004a), Astral Symbology on Iranian Coinage, *East and West* 54, pp. 31-53.

_____. (2004b), Monete dell'Iran preislamico dal Medagliere del Museo Civico Archeologico di Bologna: catalogo e considerazioni in margine, *Schools of Oriental Studies and the Development of Modern Historiography*, Melammu Symposia IV, eds. A. Panaino & A. Piras, Milano, pp. 133-159 (Pls. XVII-XVIII).

_____. (2005), Agathias e l'origine di Ardašir, *Scritti in onore di Giovanni M. D'Erme*, a cura di M. Bernardini e N.L. Tornesello, Vol. 1, Napoli, pp. 489-503.

_____. (2006), *Il regno di Xusraw dall'anima immortale. Riforme economiche e rivolte sociali nell'Iran sasanide del VI secolo*, Milano.

_____. (at press), The Role of Gold and Silver in the Sasanian Economy, *V European Conference of Iranian Studies*, Ravenna (6-11 October 2003).

Gaube, H. (1973), *Arabosasanidische Numismatik*, Braunschweig.

Genito, B. (2001), Produzione figurativa di periodo sasanide: la Via della Seta e l'Impero centralizzato, *Antica Persia. I tesori del Museo Nazionale di Tehran e la ricerca italiana in Iran*, Roma, pp. 131-143.

Ghirshman, R. (1962), *Arte Persiana. Parti e Sassanidi*, Milano.

Gignoux, Ph. (1984), *Le Livre d'Ardā Vīrāz. Translittération, transcription et traduction du texte pehlevi*, Paris.

_____. (1986), *Noms propres sassanides en moyen-perse épigraphique*. Iranisches Personennamenbuch. Band II/2, Wien.

_____. (1990), Les nouvelles monnaies de Shāpūr II, *Studia Iranica* 19, pp. 195-204.

_____. (2000), A propos de l'*airiiana vaējah*, *Studia Iranica* 29/2, pp. 163-166.

Gnoli, Gh. (1966), Un'iconografia sassanide di Zoroastro?, *Annali dell'Istituto Orientale di Napoli* 16, pp. 275-278.

_____. (1971), Politica religiosa e concezione della regalità sotto i Sasanidi, *La Persia nel Medioevo*. Accademia Nazionale dei Lincei, Roma, pp. 225-251.

_____. (1985), The Quadripartition of the Sasanian Empire, *East and West* 35, pp. 265-270.

_____. (1989), *The Idea of Iran: An Essay on its Origin*. Serie Orientale Roma LXII, Roma.

_____. (1991), L'Iran antico e lo Zoroastrismo, *L'uomo indoeuropeo e il Sacro. Trattato di antropologia del Sacro diretto da Julien Ries*, 2 Vols., Milano, pp. 105-147.

_____. (1996), Il nome degli Alani nelle iscrizioni sassanidi: considerazioni linguistiche e storiche sul tema dell'opposizione tra Iran esterno e Iran interno, *Il Caucaso: cerniera fra culture dal Mediterraneo alla Persia (secoli IV-XI)*, Settimane di Studio del Centro Italiano di Studi sull'Alto Medioevo 43, Spoleto, pp. 831-866.

_____. (1998), L'Iran tardoantico e la regalità sasanide, *Mediterraneo Antico*, I, 1, pp. 115-139.

_____. (1999), Farr(ah), *Encyclopaedia Iranica* IX, Costa Mesa, CA, pp. 312-319.

_____. (2000), *Zoroaster in History*. UCLA. Los Angeles.

Gnoli, T. (2000), *Roma, Edessa e Palmira nel III sec. D.C. Problemi istituzionali*, Pisa –Roma.

Göbl, R. (1954), Zu einigen Fälschungen vorislamischer orientalischer Münzen, *Mitteilungen der Österreichischen Numismatischen Gesellschaft* 11, pp. 1-4.

_____. (1964), Der mehrfache Münzbildrand und die numismatischen Beziehungen zwischen Byzanz und dem Sasanidenreich, *Jahrbuch der Österreichischen Byzantinischen Gesellschaft* 13, pp. 103-117.

_____. (1971), *Sasanian Numismatics*, Braunschweig.

_____. (1974), *Der Triumph des Sāsāniden Šahpuhr über die Kaiser Gordianus, Philippus und Valerianus. Die ikonographische Interpretation der Felsreliefs*, Wien.

_____. (1976), *A Catalogue of Coins from Butkara I* (Swāt, Pakistan), Rome.

_____. (1978), *Antike Numismatik*, München.

_____. (1983a), Sasanian Coins, *The Cambridge History of Iran* 3 (1), Cambridge, pp. 322-336.

_____. (1983b), Die Titel der ersten beiden Sāsāniden auf ihren Münzen, *Anzeiger der Österreichischen Akademie der Wissenschaften* 120, pp. 290-298.

_____. (1984), *System und Chronologie der Münzprägung des Kušānreiches*, Wien.

Gordus, A.A. (1995), Neutron Activation Analysis of Microgram Samples of Sasanian Coins and Metallic Art, *Material Issues in Art and Archaeology IV. Material Research Society Symposium Proceedings*, Vol. 352, Pittsburgh.

Gorini, G. (2002), L'immagine del potere nelle emissioni delle regine ellenistiche, Atti dell'incontro di studio "Sovranità e ritratto monetale", *Rivista Italiana di Numismatica* 103, pp. 307-318.

Gray, L.H. (1929), *The Foundations of the Iranian Religions*, Bombay.

Grierson, Ph. (1960), The Monetary Reforms of 'Abd al-Malik: their Metrological Basis and their Financial Repercussions, *Journal of Economic and Social History of the Orient*, pp. 241-264.

_____. (1982), *Byzantine Coins*, London.

Gurnet, F. (1994a), Deux notes à propos du mannayage de Xusrō II, *Revue Belge de Numismatique* 140, pp. 25-41 (Pl. 4).

_____. (1994b), La première émission monétaire de Valkāš, *Studia Iranica* 23, pp. 279-283.

_____. (1995), Une drachme sassanide de Peroz II, *Studia Iranica* 24, pp. 291-294.

_____. (1999), Quelques considérations sur le monnayage sassanide de Xusrō II avec *āfid* à partir de l'étude de trésors, *Matériaux pour l'histoire économique du monde iranien*, textes réunis par R. Gyselen et M. Szuppe, Cahier de Studia Iranica 21, Paris, pp. 101-122.

Gyselen, R. (1979), Ateliers monétaires et cachets officiels sasanides, *Studia Iranica* 8/2, pp. 189-212.

_____. (1984), *Une collection de monnaies de cuivre arabo-sasanides*, Studia Iranica. Cahier 2, Paris.

_____. (1989a), *La géographie administrative de l'empire sassanide. Les témoignages sigillographiques*, Res Orientales I, Paris.

_____. (1989b), Ateliers monétaires et organisation administrative sassanides, *Proceedings of the 10th International Congress of Numismatics*, London 1986, pp. 517-525.

_____. (1989c), Note de métrologie sassanide: les drahms de Khusrō II, *Revue Belge de Numismatique* 135, pp. 5-23.

_____. (1997), Economy III-IV. In the Sasanian Period, *Encyclopaedia Iranica* VIII/I, Costa Mesa, CA, pp. 104-107.

_____. (2000a), Un dieu nimbé de flammes d'époque sassanide, *Iranica Antiqua* 35, pp. 291-314.

_____. (2000b), *Arab-Sasanian Copper Coinage*, Wien.

_____. (2001), *The Four Generals of the Sasanian Empire: Some Sigillographic Evidence*, Conferenze IsIAO 14, Roma.

_____. (2002), *Nouveaux matériaux pour la géographie historique de l'empire sassanide: sceaux administratifs de la collection Ahmad Saeedi*, Cahier de Studia Iranica 24, Paris.

_____. (2003), *Dīwān* et «Trésorerie» sassanides: premières attestations sigillographiques, *Studia Iranica* 32/1, pp. 123-126.

_____. (2004), New Evidence for Sasanian Numismatics: the Collection of Ahmad Saeedi, *Contributions à l'histoire et la géographie historique de l'empire sassanide*, éd. R. Gyselen, Res Orientales XVI, Bures-sur-Yvette, pp. 49-72.

Harmatta, J. (1976), Two Economic Documents from the Sāsānian Age, *Oikumene* 1, Budapest, pp. 225-237.

Head, B.V. (1911), *Historia Numorum* (sic!), Oxford.

Henning, W.B. (1961), A Sasanian Silver Bowl from Georgia, *Bulletin of the School of Oriental and African Studies*, pp. 353-356.

Herrmann, G. (1989), *Iranische Denkmaler. Reihe II: Iranische Felsreliefs I. The Sasanian Rock Reliefs at Naqsh-i Rustam*, Berlin.

Huyse, Ph. (1999), *Die dreisprachige Inschrift Šābuhrs I. an der Ka'ba-i Zardušt (ŠKZ)*, Bd. I-II, Corpus Inscriptionum Iranicarum, Part. III. Pahlavi Inscriptions, London.

_____. (2006), Die sasanidische Königstitulatur: Eine Gegenüberstellung der Quellen, *Ērān ud Anērān. Studien zu den Beziehungen zwischen dem Sasanidenreich und der Mittelmeerwelt*, hrsg. von J. Wiesehöfer und Ph. Huyse, Oriens et Occidens Band 13, München, pp. 181-201.

Kolesnikov, A. (1999), The Quantity of Silver Coinage and Levels of Revenues in Late Sasanian Iran, *Matériaux pour l'histoire économique du monde iranien*, textes réunis par R. Gyselen et M. Szuppe, Cahier de Studia Iranica 21, Paris, pp. 123-130.

Lafaurie, J. (1964), Imitation d'un solidus de Phocas frappé par les Sassanides, *Bulletin de la Société Française de Numismatique* 19/10, pp. 412-415.

La Guardia, R. (1985), *La "Corrispondenza" Extra-Ufficio del Gabinetto Numismatico di Brera* (1805-1851), Milano.

Loginov S.D. & Nikitin A.B. (1993), Sasanian Coins of the late 4th-7th Centuries from Merv, *Mesopotamia* 28, pp. 271-296.

Lukonin, V.G. (1983), Political, Social and Administrative Institutions: Taxes and Trade, *The Cambridge History of Iran* 3 (2), Cambridge, pp. 681-746.

Macdermot, B.C. (1954), Roman Emperors in the Sasanian Reliefs, *Journal of Roman Studies* 44, pp. 76-80.

MacKenzie, D.N. (1971), *A Concise Pahlavi Dictionary*, London.

Macuch, M. (2004), Pious Foundations in Byzantine and Sasanian Law, *Convegno Internazionale: La Persia e Bisanzio*, Atti dei Convegni Lincei 201, Roma, pp. 181-196.

Malek, H.M. (1993), A Survey of Research on Sasanian Numismatics, *The Numismatic Chronicle* 153, pp. 227-269.

_____. (1995a), The Coinage of the Sasanian King Kawād II (AD. 628), *The Numismatic Chronicle* 155, pp. 119-129 (Pls. 22-24).

_____. (1995b), The Dābūyid Ispahbads of Tabaristān, *American Journal of Numismatics*, Second Series 5-6 (1993-94), pp. 105-160 (Pls. 11-17).

_____. (1996), A Hoard Group of Drachms of the Dābūyid Ispahbads and Early Abbāsid Governors of Tabaristān, *The Numismatic Chronicle* 156, pp. 175-191 (Pls. 25-32).

Malek H.M. & Curtis V.S. (1998), History of the Coinage of the Sasanian Queen Bōrān (AD. 629-631), *The Numismatic Chronicle* 158, pp. 113-119 (Pls. 33-37).

Mas'ūdī, *Kitāb al-tanbīh wa-l-išrāf. Le livre de l'avertissement et de la revision.* Traduction par B. Carra de Vaux, Société Asiatique, Paris 1896.

MHD (*Mādayān ī Hazār Dādestān*) = Perikhanian A. (1997), *The Book of a Thousand Judgements. A Sasanian Law-Book,* Costa Mesa, CA.

Miles, G.C. (1959), *Excavation Coins from the Persepolis Region,* Numismatic Notes and Monographs 143, New York.

Mochiri, M.I. (1972), *Études de numismatique iranienne sous les Sassanides,* Tome I, Teheran.

_____. (1977), *Étude de numismatique iranienne sous les Sassanides et Arabe-Sassanides,* Tome II, Teheran (revised edition, Leiden 1983).

_____. (1985), À propos d'une médaille d'or de la reine Bōrān, *Studia Iranica* 14/2, pp. 241-243.

_____. (1991), Titulature de Shāpūr II, *Iran* 29, pp. 13-22 (Pls. III-VII).

_____. (1998a), Réemploi de coins des monnaies sassanides, *The Numismatic Chronicle* 158, pp. 103-111 (Pls. 29-32).

_____. (1998b), Les monnaies de Kawād I à double effigie. *Proceedings of the Third European Conference ·of Iranian Studies,* Part I, Wiesbaden, pp. 45-54.

Morony, M. (1995), Sāsānides, *Encyclopédie de l'Islam,* Tome IX, Leiden, pp. 73-87.

Morrison, C. (1993), Les usages monétaires du plus vil des métaux: le plomb, Convegno Internazionale di Studi

Numismatici, «*Moneta e non Moneta*», *Rivista Italiana di Numismatica* 95, pp. 79-101.

Mosig-Walburg, K. (1994), Die sogenannten "Anfangsprägungen" des Kavād I und des Xusrō I, *Studia Iranica* 23/1, pp. 37-57.

_____. (1997a), Münzen des Yazdgard I. ein Beitrag zur Ikonographie, *Studia Iranica* 26/1, pp. 7-16.

_____. (1997b), Zu einige Prägungen sasanidischer Herrscher, *Iranica Antiqua* 32, pp. 209-232.

Nikitin A. & Roth G. (1995a), The earliest Arab-Sasanian Coins, *The Numismatic Chronicle*, pp. 131-138.

Nikitin A. & Roth G. (1995b), A New Seventh-Century Countermark with a Sogdian Inscription, *The Numismatic Chronicle*, pp. 277-279.

Nikitin, A. (1999), Notes on the Chronology of the Kushano-Sasanian Kingdom, *Coins, Art and Chronology. Essays on the Pre-Islamic History of the Indo-Iranian Borderlands*, M. Alram & D. E. Klimburg-Salter eds., Wien, pp. 259-263.

Nöldeke, Th. (1879), *Geschichte der Perser und Araber zur Zeit der Sasaniden. Aus der arabischen Chronik des Tabari übersetz und mit ausführlichen Erläuterungen und Ergänzungen versehn*, Leiden [reprint 1973].

Panaino, A. (1999), The Cardinal Asterisms in the Sasanian Uranography, *La Science des Cieux. Sages, mages, astrologues*, Res Orientales XII, Bures-sur-Yvette, pp. 183-190.

_____. (2000), La grande iscrizione trilingue di *Šābuhr* alla *Ka'ba-i Zardušt*. A proposito di una recente edizione, *Mediterraneo Antico* 3, 1, pp. 23-39.

_____. (2003a), The Baγān of the Fratarakas: Gods or "divine" Kings?, *Religious themes and texts of pre-Islamic Iran and Central Asia. Studies in honour of Professor Gherardo Gnoli on the occasion of his 65th birthday on 6th Decem-*

ber 2002, edited by C. Cereti, M. Maggi & E. Provasi, Wiesbaden, pp. 265-288.

_____. (2003b), Once again upon Middle Persian **māzdēsn*, *Paitimāna: Studies in Honor of Hans-Peter Schmidt*, Costa Mesa, CA, pp. 321-327.

_____. (2004a), Astral Characters of Kingship in the Sasanian and Byzantine Worlds, *Convegno Internazionale: La Persia e Bisanzio*, Atti dei Convegni Lincei 201, Roma, pp. 555-594.

_____. (2004b), La Chiesa di Persia e l'Impero Sasanide. Conflitto e Integrazione, *Cristianità d'Occidente e Cristianità d'Oriente (secoli VI-XI)*, Settimane di Studio del Centro Italiano di Studi sull'Alto Medioevo 51, Spoleto, pp. 765-869.

_____. (2006), Women and Kingship. Some Remarks about the Enthronisation of Queen Bōrān and her Sister **Āzarmīgduxt, *Ērān ud Anērān. Studien zu den Beziehungen zwischen dem Sasanidenreich und der Mittelmeerwelt*, hrsg. von J. Wiesehöfer und Ph. Huyse, Oriens et Occidens Band 13, München, pp. 221-240.

Paruk, F.D.J. (1924), *Sasanian Coins*, Bombay.

Passera, L. (2002), La circolazione monetaria nel Friuli settentrionale in epoca altomedievale (secc. VI-X), *Rivista Italiana di Numismatica* 103, pp. 93-114.

Peck, H.E. (1993), Crown, ii: From the Seleucids to the Islamic conquest, *Encyclopaedia Iranica* VI, Costa Mesa, CA, pp. 407-418.

Piras, A. (2000), La corona e le insegne del potere nell'impero persiano, *La corona e i simboli del potere*, Rimini, pp. 7-29.

_____. (2001), I Germani nell'iscrizione sassanide *Res gestae divi Saporis*, *Wentilseo. I Germani sulle sponde del Mare Nostrum*, Padova, pp. 71-82.

Raffaelli, E.G. (2001), *L'oroscopo del Mondo*, Milano.

Raschke, M.G. (1978), New Studies in Roman Commerce with the East, *Aufstieg und Niedergang der römischen Welt*, Band II, 9/2, Berlin – New York, pp. 604-1233.

Rubin, Z. (1995), The Reforms of Khusro Anūshirwān, *The Byzantine and Early Islamic Near East. III. States, Resources and Armies*. Edited by Averil Cameron, Princeton, pp. 227-297.

_____. (2002), *Res Gestae Divi Saporis*: Greek and Middle Iranian in a Document of Sasanian Anti-Roman Propaganda, *Bilinguism in Ancient Society*, ed. by J.N. Adams, M. Janse & S. Swain, Oxford, pp. 267-297.

Savio A. & Della Ferrara G. (1990), Il poliedrico Gaetano Cattaneo fondatore del Gabinetto Numismatico di Brera, *Archivio Storico Lombardo*, pp. 347-374.

Schippmann, K. (1990), *Grundzüge der Geschichte des Sasanidischen Reiches*, Darmstadt.

Sears, S. (1999), Monetary Revision and Monetization in the Late Sasanian Empire, *Matériaux pour l'histoire économique du monde iranien*, textes réunis par R. Gyselen et M. Szuppe, Cahier de Studia Iranica 21, Paris, pp. 149-167.

Schindel, N. (2002), Eine sāsānidische Kontermarke, *Mitteilungen der Österreichischen Numismatischen Gesellschaft*, Band 42, Nr. 3, pp. 57-60.

_____. (2004), *Sylloge Nummorum Sasanidarum: Paris – Berlin – Wien. Band III/1-2. Shapur II – Kawad I*, Wien.

_____. (2005), review to: Gariboldi, A. (2003), *La monetazione sasanide nelle Civiche Raccolte Numismatiche di Milano*, Milano, *Studia Iranica* 34/2, pp. 302-306.

Sellwood, D. (1983), Numismatics, *The Cambridge History of Iran* 3 (1). *The Seleucid, Parthian and Sasanian Periods*. Ed. By E. Yarshater, Cambridge, pp. 279-321.

Shahbazi, A.S. (1993), Coronation, *Encyclopaedia Iranica* VI, Costa Mesa, CA, pp. 277-279.

Shepherd, D. (1983), Sasanian Art, *The Cambridge History of Iran* 3 (2), Cambridge, pp. 1055-1112.

Sims-Williams, N. (1999), From the Kushan-Shahs to the Arabs: New Bactrian Documents Dated in the Era of the Tochi Inscriptions, *Coins, Art and Chronology. Essays on the Pre-Islamic History of the Indo-Iranian Borderlands*, Michael Alram & Deborah E. Klimburg-Salter eds., Wien, pp. 245-258.

Skjærvø, P.O. (1997), The Joy of the Cup: A Pre-Sasanian Middle Persian Inscription on a Silver Bowl, *Bulletin of the Asia Institute* 11, pp. 93-104.

_____. (2003), The Great Seal of Pērōz, *Studia Iranica* 32, pp. 281-286.

Skjærvø P.O. & Harper P.O. (1993), The Earliest Datable Inscription on a Sasanian Bowl: Two Silver Bowls in the J. Paul Getty Museum, *Bulletin of the Asia Institute* 7, pp. 181-192.

Soudavar, A. (2003), *The Aura of King. Legitimacy and Divine Sanction in Iranian Kingship*, Costa Mesa, CA.

Stausberg, M. (2002), *Die Religion Zarathushtras*, Stuttgart.

Sundermann, W. (1988), Kē čihr az yazdān. Zur Titulatur der Sasanidenkönige, *Archív Orientální* 56, pp. 338-340.

Tafazzoli, A. (2000), *Sasanian Society. I Warriors. II Scribes. III Dehqāns*, New York.

Thierry, F. (1993), Sur les monnaies sassanides trouvées en Chine, *Circulation des monnaies des marchandises et des biens*, éd. R. Gyselen, Res Orientales V, Bures-sur-Yvette, pp. 89-139.

_____. (1999), Sur les monnaies des Türgesh, *Coins, Art, and Chronology*, eds. M. Alram & D.E. Klimburg-Salter, pp. 321-349, Wien.

Tyler-Smith, S. (2000), Coinage in the Name of Yazdgerd III (AD. 632-651) and the Arab Conquest of Iran, *The Numismatic Chronicle* 160, pp. 135-170 (Pls. 13-29).

Vermeule, C.C. (1956-1957), Eastern Influences in Roman Numismatic Art. AD. 200-400, *Berytus* 12, pp. 85-99.

Vickers, M. (1995), Metrological Reflections: Attic, Hellenistic, Parthian and Sasanian Gold and Silver Plate, *Studia Iranica* 24/2, pp. 163-185.

Walker, J. (1941), *A Catalogue of Arab-Sasanian Coins*, London.

Wiesehöfer, J (2001), *Ancient Persia from 550 BC to 650 AD.* London – New York².

Wolski, J. (1993), *L'empire des Arsacides*, Acta Iranica 32, Lovanii.

Wroth, W. (1903), *A Catalogue of the Greek Coins in the British Museum. Catalogue of the coins of Parthia*, London.

Yarshater, E. (1971), Were the Sasanians Heirs to the Achaemenids?, *Atti del Convegno Internazionale sul tema: la Persia nel Medioevo*, Accademia Nazionale dei Lincei, Roma, pp. 517-533.

Zaehner, R.C. (1955), *Zurvan: A Zoroastrian Dilemma*, Oxford.

Index